Two Shades of Color

TWO SHADES OF COLOR

A Novel by
Fla' She

IamFlaShe Publishing, LLC

Published by IamFlaShe Publishing, LLC
Front Cover Photo by Frederick "Steven" Price of Slash Photography
Front Cover Design by Johnas Andre
Back Cover Design by Je' Designs Graphx
Back Cover Photo by David Lace
Edited by Sharon D. Smith

Keyword: Fla' She

To submit questions, comments, or concerns about this book or for information
about bulk purchase discounts, please send an email to:
Flashe@iamflashe.com or Iamflashe@gmail.com
Or visit www.iamflashe.com

DEDICATION

$\mathcal{I}$ dedicate this book to my beautiful grandparents, Mary Bell and Roy Lee Brown. Thank you for allowing me to be who I am and for blessing me with a giving heart and a strong mind. I love you both unconditionally. You are forever missed.

Acknowledgements

"Too often you allow external forces or people to intrude on your peace of mind and happiness. But you cannot control outside occurrences, including what other people say or do. The people who are happiest in life know this and live it. Think of it as putting a filter in your brain that only allows in positive or constructive thoughts. Tonight, celebrate a new beginning as you continue to move along a more inspiring path." *Daily Horoscope By: Max Birshtok*

With that said, I'm open for growth and prosperity. It has taken me 27 years to understand the importance of self love and respect. I know now that if I love me and my own flaws, I can not be broken. Someone will always have something to say, whether it be negative or positive. It's called an opinion. Feel free to give your judgment, but at the end of the day, I will do what makes me happy.

I give my utmost respect to God up above, for you are the only one who knows what I can endure. Thank you for loving me always, blessing me with this opportunity, and for uplifting my spirits when all else failed. You are always on time. I love you.

Mommy (Doris B. Fontenot) I love you unconditionally. You're the strongest person I know, and I'm honored to have you as my mother. Over time I watched you grow mentally and spiritually. Your compassion, independence, maternal instincts, and your strengths impress me. You are the perfect mother anyone could ask for. I appreciate your sternness when I needed it most. I wouldn't change a thing.

Daddy (Donnary L. Fontenot Sr.) I wish that we could have spent more time together over the years, but I love you as if you were by my side every day of my life. I will always be Daddy's Little Girl.

Pooby (Christyan Hall) I love you for being my #1 supporter and for encouraging me to follow what I desired. Thank you for allowing me time alone to write, and for pushing me when I thought I had writer's block. I cherish your friendship and our relationship. I love you forever and a day.

Brother (Donnary L. Fontenot Jr.) I love you for being my role model. I will never forget the Nintendo, my first cell phone, the dance videos, and the music you introduced to me as a kid. Thank you for the exposure outside of Bunkie. I love you Raye!

Sister- in- Law (Sharon J. Fontenot) thank you for being such a wonderful mother to my niece and nephew, for loving my brother unconditionally, teaching me the basics of cooking, and for finding the time to research things for me. I am truly grateful for everything, and I will never take your kindness for granted. Leah and Trey, TiTi loves you both very much.

Sister (Ursula Da- Silva) what a great inspiration you are! I want to be just like you when I grow up. (smile) Thank you for my first car, (it was my baby) and for being the sweetest lady I know. I love you and my nephews Nigel and Christian Cole.

Brother- in- Law (Chris Da- Silva) thank you for giving my sister the love and respect she deserves. You have raised a beautiful family.

MaMa (Bernita Fontenot) I love you. Thanks for all the good laughs and perfect homemade dishes. The whole family treasures them.

To all my fabulous aunts and handsome uncles, I love you all dearly.

Ms. Debbie, I love you like you were my own mother.

Amelia Wickliffe- Collins (God-Sister/ Cousin) I'm grateful for having you. Thanks for taking care of Momma when we are unable to, and for always showing me love regardless of the decisions I've made.

To my best friends/ sisters in the world: Tonya "Tee" Frazier and Constance "Connie" Trahan, thank you for always being so loyal, motivating, and supportive when I felt like saying forget everything. You have proven that true friends do exist.

To my favorite cousins, Ryan and Roy Brown, Quianna Noel, DeMaria Simmons, Kenisha Bazile, Ashley "Big A" Walker, Annie Campbell, Tonya Gordon, Kandice Bush, Ericka Myers, Kimberly and Jason Holmes, and Velna George thanks for the wonderful and crazy memories, we all need to catch up.

To my best fashion forward homegirls/ home boy, Kim Sweazie, we have to get together soon girl so we can act a fool to Miss Fiya Red ☺. I miss you. Erica Travis I miss you sweetz, I hope all is well. David "Jason" Tate don't hurt them Bro!☺;

Quentetta and LaTessa Robinson, Kimberly Joseph we go way back, Class of '01 friends since '88.

Rholanda Moore, Veronica Botley, Tamara McGhee, Donna Burks-Price, Lakeyta "Kela" Hayes, Chanae Jones, Shalyn and Shawn Lewis, Gabrielle Smith, Kimberlee Lee-Wright, Chai Hayes, Yolanda Texada, Precious "Pre-cautious," Kimberly Robinson, and Ashlie Charles it's time for a reunion.

To my Atlanta clique, and new friendships, Fredericka Jackson, Narissa Allen, Monique Ballard, Yael Naggar, Cherrian Levy, La Tasha Smith, Rosa Arias, Kristina Bulluck, Brionne Edwards, Stefany Richards, Kiah Releford, Frances Mcconell, Lennon "Chen" Johnson, Paris McQueen, Linwood "Buttons" Whitten, Elizabeth Denardo, and

Nichole Dennis thanks for fun times and the support.

To the Angel watching over me, Lalita "Lo" Gallien thank you for your lessons, love, and support.

A warm shout out to Bunkie (my home town) Chestnut for life☺, Baton Rouge (Southern University A&M College, my alma mater), and Dallas.

A very BIG thanks to all my closest friends and family, classmates, colleagues, distant friends, and past associates for gifting me with your life stories. Your stories inspired me to write this one.

Frederick "Steven" Price thanks for your hard work and dedication to the photo shoot. You're already on top. Jasmine Nicole Martinez thank you for my hot hairstyles and for gracing my book cover with your beauty. Jennifer "Je" Wilford thanks for your time and always flawless projects. Johnas "Jay" Andre your work impresses me. You were right. Quality is always better. Ms. Deloris Burks Lewis thanks for taking time out to help me with editing my synopsis and for encouraging me to continue to do better. Alton Allen thanks for the book advice and for finding the time to give me positive feedback.

I am forever gracious to everyone who inspired me and/or assisted me throughout my book writing journey. It was all worth it.

WHAT PEOPLE ARE SAYING...

After just reading the prologue, I knew <u>Two Shades of Color</u> would be one that I couldn't put down. The story captivates you from the very beginning and keeps you wanting to know more. This story can very well be the voice hidden in some of our lives, because at some point, we all have been "Color"...2 Thumbs up.

-- Jennifer 'Je' Wilford,
Author of <u>Blessed: Therapy</u>

<u>Two Shades of Color</u> is a realistic, fascinating, and challenging [book] for both men and women of all ages...whose experiences in life have taught them how not to think of themselves as a victim of circumstance, but rather to see themselves as savvy enough to select the paths that they will walk... The book begins with a mental and visual sense of raw, sensual, penetrating sex that leaves nothing to the imagination. It keeps the reader on edge and longing for more. "Color" is appreciated as a character because she learned from her unfortunate childhood experience; it made her emotionally stronger, smarter, and allowed her to survive and not be self-destructive. The metaphoric distinction of her character shows the reader that "Color" has learned that life is for the living.

-- Deloris Burks Lewis

This was an intriguing read. <u>Two Shades of Color</u> is...well articulated.

-- Alton Allen

<u>Two Shades of Color</u>, the debut erotic novel by Atlanta author, Fla' She, is...a story shared by many of us in some way...Fla' She does an excellent job at creating a very dynamic character, one who readers can relate to on many levels. Color's transition from a very challenge-filled childhood to adulthood can not be overlooked... Although Fla' She does a good job in her portrayal of Color and other key figures, readers must be strongly cautioned. Two Shades is full of risqué language and some violent scenes. However, readers who want an escape from the mundane and traditional storyline will find Two Shades to be a true page-turner.

--Sharon D. Smith, Author of
<u>Love and Liberation</u>, <u>Strapped</u>, and <u>Still Strapped</u>

PROLOGUE

His filthy hands brushed against my nipples and I pulled away in disbelief.

"Come here, Color. I have something to show you."

I looked at Carlos with fear in my eyes.

"Don't worry, I won't hurt you. You know that," he told me.

"Then why are you doing this?" I frantically asked when he kissed the nape of my neck.

"I love you and you love your Daddy C., right?" he asked trying to persuade me.

He grabbed my trembling hand and placed it on his private area.

"Daddy C you're scaring me," I said while trying to remove my hand. "Let go of me!" I yelled.
He placed his finger over his mouth, signaling for me to hush.

"Your mother is trying to sleep!" he said in a stern

voice. You don't want to wake her. She'll be real upset," Carlos reminded me. I thought about Momma resting peacefully in their bedroom.

"But you just -" I stuttered.

"You and your mother belong to me," he whispered. "I can do as I please, and you will obey. I'm the adult and you are just a kid."

I held my head down and remained quiet. I wasn't sure what he wanted, but I didn't like it one bit.

"That's a good girl," he said as he stood in front of my bed massaging his private part with my hand. He unzipped his black pants and out popped his ding a ling. I looked away quickly and shut my eyes.

"That's right, Color. You feel how strong Daddy C is?" he asked. "That's how you make me feel. Strong," he said.

With his penis in my left hand and his right hand squeezing the back of my neck, I cried silently. Carlos made faint moaning noises as he guided my hand with his.

"Ooh Angel, you are good at this," he whispered, moving my hand up and down the shaft of his penis. My body was shaking, fearing what was next. He continued to make strange noises, causing me to become more uncomfortable than before.

"Right there, Little Angel," he whispered, "right there."

Up and down and up and down, first slow now fast motions. It was weird and unfamiliar. Suddenly, Carlos released somewhat of a loud scream and something wet and sticky ran down my hand and thighs. He passed me my pillowcase and told me to wipe myself with it. It grossed me out, making me feel dirty and uneasy.

Pulling my neck towards his penis, Carlos said,

"Taste Daddy C."

"No!" I said shaking my head and folding my lips, preventing him from getting in.

"Come on Little Angel. It isn't difficult," he whispered. "I'll help you."

"No!" I told him again. Pissed off and irritated, Carlos put my princess chair up against my bedroom door, blocking anyone from entering. He then pulled me from my bed, forcing me to kneel down on the floor. Scared and confused, I obeyed him.

He positioned his body in front of me and demanded that I taste his juices.

"I don't want to Daddy C. I'm sleepy."

"Come on Color; show Daddy C how much you love him."

"No," I repeated.

He was frustrated. The nightlight in my bedroom was my focal point. I didn't want to take my eyes off of it, frightened by what he would do next.

"You will do what I tell you," he said.

He rubbed his penis around my mouth and forced my lips apart with the strength of his erect penis. He pushed my head back and forth aggressively while I cried and choked, hoping this would soon be over.

"Mmmm, Color," he said relieving himself.

Tears filled my eyes. I didn't understand why Daddy C was doing this to me. I was afraid and disappointed. I gasped for air and sniffled as tears rolled down my face and neck. I couldn't catch my breath. I panicked and pushed my whole body to the floor, head first, pulling his penis down with me. I bit down on it as hard as I could.

"Ow!" Carlos screamed.

"I said No!" I shouted. Surprised and overwhelmed by my reaction, Carlos grabbed the back of my neck and began jacking off in front of me. He ejaculated in my face seconds later. His atrocious penis dangled from his boxers as he pulled my hair and forced me to my feet. Then, he leaned me over my twin-sized bed, ripped my panties from my shivering body, and stuck his finger in my vagina. It was painful and extremely uncomfortable.

"Uhn tight, just the way I like it," he said.

I started squirming in an attempt to stop him. I cried aloud and prayed to myself. I wished my mother would come to my rescue, but she never did. I wept while he pleasured himself. His moans were loud, but my cries were much louder.

After a while of fingering me, he said in a fatherly tone, "Okay, I'll let you get some sleep."

He pulled up his pants and handed me my panties. He kissed me on my forehead and said, "Good night, Little Angel. Sweet dreams," all while smiling and winking at me.

Carlos walked out of my room after putting my princess chair in its correct destination and left my bedroom door cracked open. I placed my panties underneath my pillow case, rolled over, pulled my teddy bear closer to me, and cried myself to sleep.

CHAPTER 1
Introduction of Color

Welcome to my revolving world of money, lies, sex, and deceit. Before I begin my story, allow me to introduce myself. My name is Color, Color Jade Andrews. Twenty five years young, five foot five, with a light complexion are the lucid characteristics I possess. However, I'm a bit more complicated than that. Self- reliant, confident, creative, and a self proclaimed scholar are words that describe my true character. I'm originally from Louisiana, aka "The Boot," but I grew up in Los Angeles, California. After more than ten years of being away from home, I moved back four years ago.

When I'm here in Louisiana, I get excessively motivated about future successes. I dedicate most of my time to achieving my goals. It's my breath of fresh air. I'm enrolled at Southern University A&M College as a full time student studying Fashion Design. My passion and dedication throughout the past few years have definitely improved my chances of graduating at the top of my class. Fortunately, I'm capable of paying my college tuition by working part-time as an exotic dancer at *Tits & Wings*, a spot known for its fierce, flawless dancers and its famous buffalo wings. Dancing, as well as designing the dance costumes for me and the other dancers, is the perfect legal side hustle for single mothers and students. It pays my bills and most of my tuition.

Judge me if you may, but I love what I do. Men and women are always hitting on me. Spellbound by my green eyes and my long black hair, I constantly leave them speechless and amused. I view dancing as an expressive art form. The body is something created by God and I have learned to accept my curves and appreciate my body again. When someone misleads or exposes what's meant to be pure, untouched, loved, and protected, it can destroy a person's self-esteem. Blessed with strength and knowledge, I have overcome the agony of my child abuse. I dealt with it for years, but when it crosses my mind, it ruins my spirit. To this day, I can not fathom a grown man taking advantage of an innocent child. Don't misunderstand me. I don't take what happened to me and use it as an excuse to get what I want or even to get people to treat me as a victim. To me, it was once an obstacle that hindered my ability to believe in myself. Because of my abusive background, I focus solely on me. Since the age of seventeen, I have strived to be completely independent and over the past eight years, prayer and faith helped me accept the woman I've become.

I'll graduate from college next Friday. Unfortunately, the man who means the world to me will not be there to see me strut across that stage to receive my diploma. There have been many challenges throughout my life, but the worst ever was losing my father. This story is for you Daddy. You are and will always be the greatest father ever. I love you. Sincerely, Your Little Angel.

CHAPTER 2
Growing Pains

Growing up was like living in a make-believe story. The years I spent in Louisiana were the best years of my life. So many people around me motivated me and cared for me. Our home, my father's job, and the love we all shared for one another was surreal. We lived in Baton Rouge. My mother, Helen, was a stay at home mom. She designed scrap books from time to time, but mostly she was busy being a mother and a wife. She always kept the house clean and had a hot meal cooked every day. Sometimes she would let me help her in the kitchen when she baked. She made the best cupcakes in the city. I miss my momma's cupcakes. Licking the icing from the spoon and icing the cupcakes were my favorite things to do when helping out in the kitchen. My mother was a supportive and nurturing woman. She helped me with my homework and read me bedtime stories every night. With her petite frame, gorgeous face, vanilla skin, brown eyes, and long black hair, she could have had any man she wanted. I was so glad she chose my father.

My father was a tall, handsome, dark skinned man with green eyes and wavy black hair. He worked for FedEx in New Orleans as a truck driver, which kept him on the road a lot. When he was home with us, it felt like he never really left. I enjoyed those moments. The three of us would say our blessings at the dinner table, eat our food, and then watch movies or play board games like checkers or monopoly. I never really knew what I was doing, but they always made me feel like I did.

My parents met in college during their freshmen year and had been inseparable ever since. Whenever I saw the two of them together, it made my heart skip a beat. Their connection was amazing. The look in their eyes when they interacted with each other was so authentic. It made me imagine how I would live my life with my husband and children when I grew up. I pictured my husband being as handsome and hardworking as my daddy. Just Daddy's smile would light up the room. When he came home from work, he'd tickle me, then pick me up and pretend he was going to let me fall from his arms.

He called me his Little Angel. Daddy taught me how to tie my shoelaces, ride a bicycle, skate, and how to play a little basketball and softball. Sometimes he would get a little too rough with me and my mother would get all nervous if she heard me crying. I cried a few times, but he would always tell me to suck it up. After a few bruises and scraped knees, I took heed to what he was teaching me.

One day my mom and I were sitting in the living room watching *The Cosby Show* and there was a knock at the front door.

"Oh your father must have misplaced his keys again," my mother said.

I began to get real anxious about seeing Daddy. I had so much to tell him. Momma got up to answer the door. Minutes later I heard her scream, "God, no not my Royal!"

I panicked. Suddenly, I felt a lump in my throat. I ran to the door only to find two officers trying to console my mother as she fell to her knees. Momma grabbed me.

"He's gone, Baby," she said as she sobbed. "Your daddy isn't coming home."

Tears trickled down my face onto her pina colada scented hair. From that point on, my life hasn't been the same. The policemen said Daddy was driving home when a teenage girl threw her newborn baby out of her moving car. He slammed on breaks to avoid running the baby over and drove across a median into oncoming traffic. His car flipped over twice, breaking his neck. He was killed instantly.

I was nine at the time of the tragedy. My mother didn't take his death very well. In the beginning, she stopped being herself completely. The happiness and joy she had when Daddy was alive had all died with him. She wouldn't eat, she quit cooking, and it seemed as though she just stopped living. The phone rang off the hook with calls from concerned friends, but she never answered. Momma was in a daze for about eight months.

Then one day I noticed the drastic change. When I came home from school, she was sitting on the couch watching their wedding video. I heard the video playing before I stepped foot into the living room to see her face. I expected her to be crying, but instead her eyes were filled with joy and peace again.

"Momma, are you okay?" I asked.

"Yes, Baby. Momma's okay." She smiled at me while she touched my faced. "Have a seat, Color. I want to talk to you."

"Yes, Momma," I replied.

"I'm at peace with things now, Baby," she said. "Your father came to me in my dream and reminded me that I have you and I was not alone. He said to cherish our good moments and not to worry about him."

My hands shook because I knew every word my mother was saying was true.

"Baby, I'm sorry for neglecting you all this time," she said emotionally.

"It's okay, Momma."

"No Color, it isn't. It's just us now and I'm confident when I say that your father will live on in our spirits."

I hugged her really tight and told her that Daddy had come to me months ago and asked me to take care of her, too. She smiled at me as if all the pain had gone away.

Three months later, Momma got a job offer in Los Angeles, working as a Business Administrator. She had a Bachelor of Science degree in Business Management, but I never knew my mother to work a real job before. I later found out that she worked for an investment company for three years before she got pregnant with me. When we first arrived in Los Angeles, we moved in with her college roommate Deloris and her kids Kelly and Kendle. It was real fun at first, but after a few months of fighting over dolls, food, and clothes, Momma realized we needed our own place. We moved into a two-bedroom loft in downtown L.A., which was much closer to my mother's job. I loved it a whole lot and we felt like it was a fresh start for both of us.

I attended private school near our home, which took a little getting used to since I went to public school all of my life. I met some new friends, however, at school named Fallon and Monica. They both were very nice and welcoming. We helped each other with homework and took turns having play dates. Fallon was Black and Hispanic with long, dark hair braided down her back. She was very thin and much taller than most kids our age. We met outside on the playground. She was climbing the monkey bars as I walked to the other end to play on the swings. She walked over to me and introduced herself.

"Hey," she said. "What's your name?"

"I'm Color," I replied. "What's your name?"

"I'm Fallon, or Fal for short. Where are you from?" she asked.

"I'm from here," I lied.

"No you're not," she commented. "I saw your mom bring you here just the other day when Sister Mary gave you and your mom a tour of the school," she said.

"I'm from Louisiana," I told her.

"Louisiana!" she shouted. "That's a long way from here."

I shook my head and agreed with her.

"You can play with me if you want," she said.

Fal and I talked as we played. She told me her favorite color was green and she didn't mind getting dirty, unlike Monica and I.

Monica, or Mo as we called her, was prissy and loved makeup. She was half Black and half White. She wore her sandy colored hair down most of the time and everything she owned was pink. Mo and I met my first day of school. The teacher introduced us and told me that

Monica would be showing me around until I got the hang of things.

"Welcome to St. Mary's," she said and reached her hand out to me.

"Thank you," I replied as I shook her hand.

"Have you ever been in private school before?" she asked.

"No, but it seems fun."

"I wouldn't call it fun just yet." she replied.

"Why?" I asked.

"You haven't met Sister Anne."

"Who's Sister Anne?" I asked out of curiosity.

"You will meet her later on today. She's over Mass."

I was thankful I met Mo before meeting Sister Anne, who didn't mind confronting any of us in front of the whole student body if we misbehaved.

Mo and I played dress up and Fal and I played basketball and softball. Fal was a tomboy and Mo and I were becoming young ladies. Even though Fal and Mo's personalities clashed, all three of us eventually became best friends. As I made friends, so did my momma. She met other women and guys with kids. After a few months, our new life felt like a great new beginning.

CHAPTER 3
My Worst Nightmare

Two years after my father's passing, Momma started dating this guy at her office named Ralph. This man literally had the same features as my father. He was tall and dark with wavy hair. He walked like him, talked like him, and he even smelled like my father. It was awkward. There was just something about him that made me not really care for him. No one could ever replace my father and my mother knew that. I assumed she only yearned for the next best thing.

After a few dates, Ralph wanted to stay overnight. Momma and Ralph ordered take out from the Japanese restaurant around the corner and we all watched two episodes of *The Cosby Show*. When the show went off, we sat around and I told them silly "yo momma" jokes. After a while of talking to them about school, my mother told me it was past my bedtime and to tell Ralph good night. It was fun entertaining them with my kiddy jokes, but I knew I couldn't stay up with them all night so I went to bed.

Later that night Momma and I found out Ralph was married to a man. Ralph was straight up gay! That was when I first discovered the true meaning of what gay really was. Momma always referred to it as being too happy, which I never really understood. That night, Ralph's husband threw a brick through my mother's windshield. Momma's car alarm went off then someone started ringing the doorbell like crazy. I'm talking DRA- MA!

I heard an unfamiliar voice shouting.

"Ralph, if you don't get your tired, lying ass down here, I will come in there and drag your black ass out!"

I hopped out of bed and looked out of my bedroom window and there was a tall, skinny Black guy standing in front of our loft with a brick in his hand.

"We are married, Ralphy and I'm tired of your bullshit! If you're not down here in 20 seconds I'm coming in!"

I heard the guy counting. "He better hurry," I remember thinking. I peeped from behind my bedroom door and saw Momma and Ralph arguing. Ralph was busy trying to explain to Momma.

"Helen he's lying! We haven't seen each other in over a month," Ralph said.

Momma grabbed her 22 pistol from the nightstand in her bedroom and told him, "Nigga get the hell out!"

Ralph seemed nervously surprised.

"I'm leaving, but I want to explain first," he said.

Momma looked over and saw me peeking out the door.

"Color, get back in your room and shut the door!"

27

Not wanting to obey, I turned away and went into my room and cracked my door just enough to eavesdrop.

"I don't want to hear shit you have to say, Ralph. You're pathetic. Get out now!"

"But it's not what you think! Let me talk to you, Baby," Ralph pleaded.

"Talk to the damn door!"

The front door soon slammed shut. Momma raced to her bedroom and then her door slammed shut. A few minutes later, she came into my room and told me she needed to talk to me about what had just happened. I came from under the covers out of curiosity.

"Baby that is the kind of unexpected drama life will bring you. Ralph was working on being a part of our family when he knew he was married! People can be so deceiving, so make sure you're aware of what may or may not deceive those beautiful eyes of yours."

I just smiled and asked, "Momma, were you really going to shoot him?" She looked at me and smiled.

"If I wasn't, his husband sure would have." We laughed and said good night.

Approximately six and a half months later, she started talking about this new guy she had met in her Yoga class named Carlos. Momma waited a while before she introduced us to each other. I guess she wanted to make sure he was legit. One Sunday evening after church, we made plans to meet him at the park for a picnic.

The park was a great place for us to meet because it was kid and adult friendly. It was during spring and the sun was shining so brightly. Most of the flowers had bloomed, the wind was blowing, and birds were chirping. Some people walked, others skated along the sidewalk, but most people sat and ate with loved ones. Momma and I sat under a large tree near a pond when Carlos approached us. We had just laid down the blanket and removed the food from the labeled containers when he walked up and covered Momma's eyes from behind.

"Guess who?" he asked, startling my mother.

"Oh, Carlos," my mother responded. He uncovered her eyes, handed her a handful of yellow lilies, and kissed her on her cheek.

"You must be, Color," he said reaching his hand out to me.

"Yes, I'm Color. Nice to meet you," I said.

"It's very nice to finally meet you young lady," he said as he joined us on the picnic blanket. When he shook my hand, I noticed the sandalwood fragrance he wore. He was average height, about 165 lbs., brown skinned, with a bald head. He sported stone washed jeans, black sandals, and a button down black shirt. My first impression of him was that he was friendly and very attentive to us both. We ate fried chicken, rice dressing, and potato salad Momma prepared. I sat there and listened as Momma and Carlos talked to each other. It wasn't much I could say at eleven years old.

When we were done eating, I sat in the car and listened to music while they went for a short walk. They looked happy together, considering they had only been dating for a short while. Carlos owned a catering business, he didn't have any children, wasn't gay, and he wasn't married. I thought Daddy would have approved.

As time passed, our relationship with Carlos grew stronger and two years later, he asked my mother to marry him. I was happy for her because she deserved to be with someone who would cater to her and treat her like the Queen she is. A month before their wedding, Carlos sold his condo and moved in with us. They thought the loft was a better investment and besides, his business and Momma's job was only a few miles away from our home so it was perfect.

My thirteenth birthday was coming up and Carlos planned for all of us, including Fal and Mo, to go to Coney Island in New York that weekend. A few days after returning home, I started calling Carlos "Daddy C." It seemed right at the time. He and my mother were both surprised, but very content with it.

Our lives had started over and I felt lucky to have my new family. However, months after calling Carlos Daddy C more frequently, I noticed him acting a little strange towards me. He would stare at me from head to toe as I walked by him and he would call me "his cheeks" when Momma wasn't around. I didn't take it out of context at first because I always had chubby cheeks. Then one evening my mom had a late meeting and Carlos came to tuck me into bed and kissed me on my lips. I'm not talking like a daddy to daughter kiss, more like a daddy to mommy kiss.

I panicked and I told him, "You shouldn't have done that!"

"I shouldn't have done what?" he asked. "I was only giving my Little Angel a kiss goodnight. This will be our little secret. Daddy C is going to take good care of you."

He left out of the room and all I could think about was how he kissed me and how he called me his "Little Angel." Daddy used to call me his Little Angel, too, when I was younger. I wondered if my Momma had told him about that. I got out of bed and fell on my knees and asked God to forgive me for my sins. Even as a young girl, I knew it was wrong, but I believed it was my fault.

"Lord please don't make my Momma unhappy again and please don't let me kiss my Daddy C on the lips anymore," I prayed. As time went on, Daddy C made frequent visits into my bedroom. The threats got worse and he started putting his hand underneath my nightgown every chance he would get. Every night I prayed and asked God for forgiveness and help. Daddy C just came around more and did more sexual things to me when Momma was either sleeping or away from home. I asked Momma for pajamas in place of my nightgowns, but she wouldn't buy me any.

Her response was, "You have always slept in nightgowns, Sweetheart. Besides, pajamas are a lot more expensive."

I wanted to cry out to her so bad, but I needed her to read between the lines. On my fifteenth birthday, my mother went away on a business trip and I stayed home alone with Carlos. I begged her to let me spend the weekend with Fal, but she said she needed to know I was okay while she was away.

"Please, Momma. I'll do chores forever if you let me stay at Fal's this weekend."

"The answer is 'no,' Color, and that's final!"

She left the day before my birthday, leaving me alone with her monster of a husband. On my birthday, Carlos had a pink and white birthday cake delivered to me with a note that said, *"Happy Birthday, Angel!!! Tonight is the night you will become a WOMAN."* Instantly I started to freak out. I didn't know what to do. I tried calling my mother's cell, but my calls were transferred to her voicemail. I panicked and wondered if I could really trust my homegirls because I wanted to tell someone. I had to. I took deep breaths and decided I'd just wait for my mom to call back and tell her everything that has happened. Well, that was not a good idea since she called right when Carlos was walking into the door from work.

With his white chef's jacket thrown neatly across his arm, the very first thing he said was, "Did you get the cake I made especially for you?"

"Yes, I got it." I said rolling my eyes. He snatched the phone from my hand, talked to Momma for a few minutes, and hung up.

"I wanted to talk to her," I told him.

"You can speak to her later. She's in a meeting now," Carlos responded.

He walked out of the living room, went into their bathroom and ran the shower. I figured since he never touched me outside of my bedroom that I would stay up and watch television in the living room until he finally fell asleep. As soon as I heard him snoring, I ran quickly into my room and put a chair behind the door. My doorknob never did have a lock on it because Momma never called a maintenance person to fix it. I dozed off for about an hour, only to wake up to Carlos leaning over me with his penis out his boxers, breathing hard, and playing with himself.

"What are you doing?" I asked as I set up in bed. He just stood there silently looking at me with his penis still in his hand.

"You know what I want, Color," he said as he stared into my eyes. I screamed as loud as I could, but he covered my face with a pillow.

"Quiet, Color! You won't feel a thing," he assured me. I tried kicking and fighting him, but he was too strong for me to handle. Carlos pulled the bed covers back, uncovering my entire body. Then he forced my leg open with his left hand and held me down by my throat with his right hand.

"Shut up and take this dick!" he yelled.

Suddenly, he ripped my panties from around me, and forced his penis inside my vagina. I couldn't breathe. I gasped for air, but I felt nothing but pain. My vagina was being torn piece by piece.

"That pussy's tight," Carlos kept saying. "Shh, good little pussy," he said while he wiped tears from my face. I couldn't control my emotions. My face was swollen and wet from crying and trying to catch my breath.

"I can't breathe," I struggled to say. "Please, I can't breathe. Please stop."

He wouldn't stop. He kept on choking and penetrating me like it was okay, like everything was normal. I thought I was dying. A part of me actually wanted to die. I wanted nothing more than for Carlos to take his sleazy hands off me. My body began to shiver. Blood was flowing down my thighs and legs onto my sheets and the floor. During that moment, I realized I had to save myself. I closed my eyes and prayed to God asking for my mother's return. I wanted her to catch her husband on top of her 15-year-old daughter against my will. I knew she would pull that 22 pistol out and protect me. Shortly after, he got off of me.

"You're officially a woman now, Angel," he said.

He walked out of my room, and I ran straight to my bathroom's shower, leaving a trail of blood behind me. Afterwards, I was unable to fall asleep. I lay awake on a blanket, crying and trembling. I was no longer a virgin. I wanted to wait until I was married, but he took that from me. And even though I wasn't responsible for his actions, I was the one who suffered. From the age of thirteen to seventeen, I was molested and sexually abused by my "Daddy C." I was forced to realize I had been betrayed by the sweet, charming man who swept my mother off her feet years ago.

The next day, I stayed in bed and Carlos didn't even try to make me go to school. Later that evening, my mother came home and I told her what happened. She cursed at me and asked how I could say such a hateful thing about Carlos.

"That man has been nothing but a father to you!" were her exact words. I was going to show her the cake and my ripped panties, but he had disposed of all the proof I could have possibly used to persuade her otherwise. I couldn't believe her. My own mother, the woman who said it was us against the world because it was full of vindictive people. I knew if I couldn't get through to her, my Momma, I was in this alone.

CHAPTER 4
State of Revenge

Carlos raped me one more time after that. Most of the time I would wake up to him standing over my bed beating his meat. I could hear him moan while he stood over me. I was just glad he stopped touching and penetrating me. I'm not sure why he stopped, but I kept a blade under my pillow just in case he made a move. If Momma didn't believe me, she'd know why he was walking out of my room with a bloody dick.

After preparing for his next move, about two years and some months later, he caught me off guard. I'd been in bed all day with bad menstrual cramps. I bled heavily and I'm not myself when I get my period. I was home alone and I decided to take a hot bath to soothe the pain. I started undressing as I waited for the bath water to fill the tub. Carlos came in and held me at gunpoint. I could smell liquor on his breath.

"Bitch if you even move an inch, I'll kill you!" he whispered. "Your momma told me your school counselor called. I figured maybe you ran your mouth and told someone about our little secret. We've kept that between us for years and now you decide to tell. You want to see your Daddy C go to jail?"

"What? Get the fuck out, Carlos!" I told him, not caring about his reaction.

"Bitch, I will kill you and make it look like you committed suicide," he told me, placing the gun against my face.

There were so many mixed emotions going on in my head. I was scared and furious. There I was on my period, helpless, and just tired of him bothering me. He even had the audacity to have my Momma's gun to my head. He ripped the rest of my clothes off, grabbed my throat and started raping me from behind, in my asshole. It hurt me so bad.

When he was done he said, "I fucked you in your ass so I wouldn't hurt that lil bloody pussy of yours."

When he left out, I laid on the bathroom floor for hours. Feeling alone and disgusted, something clicked in my head and I decided that it was time for me to take control of the situation; enough was enough.

Days later, I started thinking about vicious things I wanted to do to him. I had flashes of him touching me and all I could see was his ugly ass grin as if he was doing me a favor. I searched deep in my mind and finally came up with the perfect plan of revenge. I wanted him to experience some sort of humiliation, pain, and death. I knew people around Fallon's hood who would do just about anything for the right price.

When Daddy died, he left me forty thousand

dollars for my college tuition. I had access to twenty of it immediately and the other twenty once I turned 21. I took half of my college fund and paid some homeboys of mine $20,000 to take care of my living nightmare. I told them to torture him with a sixteen inch dildo in his ass until he shitted blood. Then, I instructed them to strip his clothes off of him and hang him from an abandoned building while the dildo hung from his ass. After they hung him from the building, I showed up with stick pins and inserted as many as I could in his limp dick. I wanted that man to suffer as much as I did.

"Let me down, Color, I'm sorry! Is that what you want me to do, apologize? I'm sorry!"

"So am I, Carlos," I told him. "I'm sorry I didn't do this sooner." He looked so scared, but I didn't care. "Who's the bitch now?" I asked. "Carlos if you scream, I'll kill you."

I reached into my handbag and pulled out the same 22 he held to my head days earlier.

"Do you think I'll kill you?" I asked.

"You don't have it in you, Bitch!"

"You're right, Carlos, I don't."

I put the 22 in my jacket pocket, and walked away. I told the boys to get him down and leave his body in an alley butt ass naked with the dildo still in his ass. They laughed and said, "Done. Any other requests before we take care of dude?"

"No just make sure he isn't breathing," I told him.

"Anything for you, Color."

It was almost as if I had personally taken care of the whole thing myself. Sad thing is, he raped three other young girls prior to me and had served a small amount of time in prison because of it. Some people may say that

$20,000 isn't enough money to take someone's life, but Carlos was an evil, twisted man who took a whole lot more from me and three other young girls. I'm accountable for what I did to him, and he was accountable for what he had done to us. I bet it never crossed his mind that one of us could easily fuck his world up in such a vengeful way.

My mother ended up having a nervous breakdown and was admitted to a psychiatric hospital. Carlos' sudden death took her by surprise. Everything was out of her hands though. It was too late for her to try and do anything about it. I believe she became overwhelmed with the situation when she found out about the other girls he was accused of raping and one rape in which he was actually convicted. I'm sure she was hurting from losing another husband, but in a sense relieved by his death. I say that because she was upset when she found out about the previous instances and thought I was just making things up for attention. I'm sure she blames herself for not preventing the situation.

I know a lot of adolescents do and say things that aren't true so they can get attention, but I was far from that. I didn't believe in telling lies that serious just to get anyone's attention. I get enough of it already. I feel bad about my mother being admitted to a psychiatric hospital. I thought that my cry for help would have been addressed by Momma, but since my cries were unheard, I had to protect myself.

CHAPTER 5
For Love & Money

I immediately started looking for a job. With my mother being gone, I had to take over most of her responsibilities. I didn't have any work experience, but those bills had to be paid. Our loft was paid for, but there were other bills we were obligated to pay such as the utilities, bus fare, phone service, insurance, and other necessities, which all exceeded a thousand dollars a month. I planned on saving for a car once I got a job. We lived downtown and there was no way any of the Fortune 500 companies and high ranked businesses would hire a non-degreed, 17 year old without any experience. I had to go further into the hood to find something.

I asked Fallon if she had any idea of who was hiring near the beach since she worked there part time as a lifeguard. She suggested I put in an application as a lifeguard, but I would have needed practice swimming first since I hadn't swam since my dad was alive. Of course I didn't want to waste time doing that. I had a month before these bills would come at me in full speed. Fal also did tattoos on the side, but I did not have the talent to help out with that. Dealing with all kinds of people was my forte, so I thought about something pertaining to customer service.

Instead of looking near my place or Fal's job, we drove to the inner city. A "now hiring" sign was posted in the window of a dry cleaners. We stopped and I filled out an application for a cashier position that was available. The owner preferred someone with previous cashier experience. I told the manager I was a quick learner and if she taught me the basics, I could handle the job. She wasn't moved by my enthusiasm and offered me a cleaning position paying $5.30 an hour bi- weekly. I didn't take it because it would have taken me forever to save for a car, not to mention my priorities. I told her I would let her know by the end of the day. When I went back into the car, I told Fal what she was offering.

She was like, "Please, $5.30 an hour for cleaning labor, I can afford to pay you more than that."

I applied at a few other places too. I was determined to get a job even two if I could manage. After driving around the city all morning and most of the afternoon, we got hungry and stopped at a black owned restaurant, an after hours club, that had opened a few weeks ago. Fal said she would treat, so I didn't argue with her decision.

When we entered the place, I was impressed with the décor. A bar sat to the right of the dining area, crystal-like chandeliers hung throughout the ceiling, hardwood floors, white tablecloths, and a stage. There was a black leather sofa in the V.I.P. area that could have possibly sat 15 people, a large dance floor in the center of the restaurant, and a DJ booth behind it.

"Now this is the kind of place you need to be working in, Color. These people are making money."

She was right. The male servers were dressed in black slacks, black button down shirts with red ties. The female servers wore black skirts with red blouses and black bow ties. I loved their outfits. They were all neatly dressed and well coordinated.

"Hi, welcome to *The Palace*. How many are in your party?"

"A party of two," I informed her. The hostess was really friendly.

"Here you are ladies, your server will be right with you. Enjoy!"

We looked through the menu after we were seated. I had a taste for shrimp pasta. Fal thought about ordering fried chicken with macaroni and cheese. Suddenly we were interrupted by the waiter.

"Good afternoon. My name is Jay and I will be serving you lovely ladies."

"What's the special of the day?" I asked him.

"The lunch special is our Jack Daniel's boneless chicken breast, served with a baked potato, mixed vegetables and your choice of soup or salad."

"Oh that sounds tasty," Fal told him.

"What would you recommend?" I asked.

"Actually I love our steaks, the fried chicken, potato salad, baked fish and our salads just to name a few."

"Dang Jay you make it all sound appealing. Give us a few minutes to look over the menu," Fal suggested.

Jay took our drink orders while Fal and I struggled to make the perfect meal selection.

"I will have those out to you shortly."

"Thank you," I said.

41

"No problem, Ms."

"Color, you should ask him if he has a girlfriend. He's cute."

"He's straight, but girl I'm more interested in finding myself a job. As a matter of fact, I'll be right back. I'm going talk to the hostess real quick and ask her if I can get an application and maybe speak with the manger."

"That's fine, but remember, I need to be back on our end no later than 5:00 pm," Fal reminded me.

"I'll be fast."

"Okay, Color do your thang!"

I walked over to the hostess.

"Excuse me, are you all hiring?" I asked.

"Yes we sure are, but we're only taking applications on Tuesdays and Thursdays from 2-4," she replied.

"Is the manager available for me to speak with?"

"No, she isn't, but the owner is."

"Great. Would it be a problem if I spoke with the owner?" I asked her.

"No, not at all. I'll send him over to your table as soon as I see him. Oh, and I'm Asia by the way."

"Thanks Asia, I'm Color."

"Color? That's a unique name."

"Thanks. It was nice talking to you," I told her.

"Same here, Color," she replied.

I headed back over to our table just in time to order the spicy shrimp pasta. Fal ended up ordering the lunch special with a side of macaroni and cheese.

"So what happened?"

"Nothing, I was just inquiring about their hiring status."

"So?"

"So, what?" I asked her.

"So are they hiring?"

"Yea, I guess."

"Well that's a good thing, right?" she asked.

"They're only taking applications Tuesdays and Thursdays though."

"What's wrong with that?"

"Today is Friday, Fal."

"Well yeah, but I can make plans ahead of time to bring you up here on Tuesday."

Before I could respond, this tall, dark, sexy, brother approached us at our table. I lost my chain of thought, my breath, and I must have lost my mind, too. I couldn't take my eyes off of him. He was gorgeous.

"Hello ladies, I understand one of you is interested in working here at my restaurant."

"Uh, yea, I mean yes, that would be me." I extended my arm for a handshake.

"Hi, I'm Color."

"My pleasure, Color. I'm Mr. Clay."

"It's nice to meet you." I told him. "This is my best friend, Fallon.

"Hi," Fal said.

"Hello," he replied.

"You have a very nice place here," Fal said to him.

"Thank you."

"So Color, which position are you interested in?"

"Whichever position you'd like." Fal tapped me on my hand.

"I'm so sorry, Mr. Clay. Actually I'm most interested in the highest paying position available.

"Now see, that may be a problem."

"Why is that?" I asked him.

"I'm currently filling that position."

"Oh, sense of humor, too, I see."

His teeth were so white, he had nice curly hair, and I knew I had fallen for my future boss.

"You're so funny," I told him.

"Seriously, Color," he said interrupting my laughter. "If you're a friendly, patient, money motivated person who loves cash every day, I would recommend starting off as a server. My hostesses are paid $10.00 an hour, cooks make $12 to $14 an hour depending on experience, and servers are paid $3.75 an hour plus tips."

"Wow, you pay pretty well."

"I strongly believe that if the employee is happy, so is the customer. Employees eat free lunch and dinner is half off."

I interrupted, "There is one concern I have."

"What is it?" he asked.

"I don't have any experience, but I'm a people's person, a fast learner, and I love money."

"You seem to be well rounded and polite enough to work a job like this. I'm going to give you a chance. Take this menu home, learn it by Tuesday morning, and I'll put you in my evening orientation class."

"Thank you, Mr. Clay."

Before he walked off, Jay arrived with our food. It looked and smelled delicious. He brought out shredded cheese, extra Jack Daniel's sauce, napkins, and refilled our drinks.

"Do you ladies need anything else?" he asked politely.

"No, Sweetheart, we're fine. Everything looks great," I told him.

"Enjoy. I'll be back to check on you soon."

"So what did you think of Mr. Clay?" I asked Fal.

"What, besides you drooling all over him?"

"I was not!"

"Any position you like," she said teasing me. We laughed.

"You must admit. The man is fine."

"He has a lot going for himself as far as we can see, but Color he's way too old for you."

"He's amazing is what I think."

"He seems cool," she suggested. "Remember what your goal is though. Don't get off track, Color. You have bills to pay now."

"Most definitely, Fal. I just need to have a little fun while I make this money."

Over the weekend, I studied the restaurant's menu and by Monday evening, I had it all memorized. Fal brought me to *The Palace* like she promised and sure enough after passing Mr. Clay's quiz, I was able to start orientation. Asia was actually the instructor for the two day orientation. We learned the values and the motto of the restaurant. She also discussed methods of approaching the customers, how to wear our uniforms, and best of all to get the big tip. It was all real intriguing. It was almost as if we were being taught how to hustle people. I started working that following Friday. It was a very busy day. I worked from eleven that morning until eight thirty that evening and I made $267. 83. I couldn't believe it. If I would have been able to stay throughout the evening I know I would have made a whole lot more. At 9pm the restaurant is transformed into a night club, but I was not old enough to serve drinks.

A few months passed and I was able to buy my first car. It was a used '97 Green Honda Accord Sedan. It didn't have a working stereo, but it ran well. Over the last eight months, I managed to save two grand of emergency money, and I was able to pay the bills on time. Asia and I became acquaintances after I covered her shift a few times.

Kenneth, also known as "Mr. Clay," was busy spoiling me. We had been dating each other for 9 weeks now. He treats me like a woman. He's always impressing me with little sweet gestures here and there, and the larger things were coming nonstop. Kenneth was very considerate and open to my opinions, which was why I was so attracted to him. It took some time getting used to since he was my first real boyfriend. I've never been catered to or cared for in such a manner. The other female servers and hostesses at work are somewhat bitter about our relationship, but who cares.

Momma was doing better and probably going to be getting out of the psychiatric hospital soon. I was anticipating the day. I hoped our relationship hadn't fallen apart due to everything that happened. I kept thinking that maybe she was blaming herself. She may have some trust issues, but we would get through it together. Momma hadn't met Ken, but I wanted to introduce them when she got home. He seemed like the kind of guy she would love for me to settle down with and marry. Ken was an independent, clean cut, handsome man. Aside from the fact that he was eleven years older than I was, I was sure everything else would get a definite approval.

CHAPTER 6
Grown Woman Shit

My 18th birthday was near and I was ecstatic. The girls and I planned a girl's night out at a strip club. I never stepped foot in one so I was looking forward to it. Ken didn't know about the strip club, but I was sure he wasn't going to mind. He was very secure and his confidence was mega high. He spent more time getting dressed than I did. He loved smelling good and looking flawless all the time. I loved that about him. Kenneth, on the other hand, had different plans for my birthday. He said he had a surprise for me.

Asia asked me to join her and my girls for lunch today to discuss a few details regarding my birthday celebration. We were meeting at this bar and grill called *Peeps*. When I arrived, Fal, Mo, Erica, Kim, and Asia were all sitting at the bar having drinks.

"What's up girls?" I asked walking up to the bar.

They all turned their tipsy behinds around with shocked expressions on their face.

"What?" I asked them. "Why are you all looking at me like that?"

"We were not expecting to see you here," Kim said.

"We were discussing the final plans for your birthday," Mo added.

"Asia said we were all meeting here today," I told them.

"Damn, Asia, do you always have to tell Color everything?" Mo asked her.

"It's cool girls, it was just a misunderstanding," I responded. "Carry on. I have a few errands to run before I head back to work anyway."

In my head, I was wondering how the hell Asia made a crazy mistake like that. I started to wonder about that girl. Fal and Mo had been my girls since I moved to Cali. Kim and I met in English class my freshmen year in high school. Erica and I met through a guy we both liked. Asia and I got closer since we started working together. She was a few years older than all of us, but she loved coming to me for advice. It's cool I like being the confidant, but I will never confide in her big mouth ass. Asia didn't like Fal for some reason, but she knows she can never disrespect Fal around me or even talk shit about her in my presence.

Before returning to work I stopped at the mall to purchase a bottle of cologne and a nice tie for my honey. He does so much for me and I wanted him to know I care about him and that everything he's done for me is greatly appreciated. I gift wrapped both his gifts and began writing in his card. I wrote: *Ken, this is a gift of appreciation from your Baby Girl. I love everything about you and I can not wait to see what's in store for us. I Love You. Love Always, Color Jade.*

He gave me a set of keys to his BMW so I thought it would be cute if I placed it on the passenger's seat. We have yet to be sexual, but we made plans to go all the way on my birthday. Technically I wasn't a virgin and he was aware of what happened between Carlos and me. My sweetheart had been so supportive of me by respecting my decision to wait.

When I pulled up at work, I didn't see Ken's car. I decided to wait and give it to him later on tonight. Before I got out of my car, Ken called me on my cell.

"Hello," I said.

"What's up, Baby Girl?" he asked. "How's your day going?"

"It's been fine, Baby. My lunch date didn't go as planned," I told him.

"That's okay, Sweetheart. I'll make it up to you. How does dinner at *Houston's* sound?" he asked.

"Baby, I was thinking about preparing dinner at my place tonight. It will be nice, I promise." I told him.

"You got that, Baby Girl. What time should I arrive?"

"7:30 sharp," I suggested.

"Okay, see you then, Sexy."

Instead of going back to work to finish out the remaining four hours of my shift, I drove over to the nearest grocery store. Ken's favorite dish was Rib eye steak and baked potatoes, so that's just what I decided to make along with mixed vegetables and a garden salad. Next I needed to find a sexy dress in one of his two favorite colors, black and blue. After I left the grocery store, I swung by *The Karma*, a boutique over on Hollywood Blvd. I was sure I could find the perfect cocktail and party dress.

I tried on a black knee length tube top dress that fit my body like a glove. It was perfect for my King.

I hurried home with just enough time to prepare dinner, take a shower, get dressed, pin my hair up, and set the table. Our wine rack was full. I served the Moscato instead of the Merlot. Soon after I lit the candles on the dinner table, he was knocking on the door. I opened the door and Ken was holding a dozen of white tulips, my favorite, in his left hand.

"These are for you, Baby Girl. Wow, you look so sexy."

"Thank you and you look mighty handsome, too," I told him.

"Ooh Wee, Color! You are wearing the hell out of that dress, Baby Girl!" he said when I turned to walk away.

"Well don't just stand there, Baby. Come in and shut the door." I placed my beautiful flowers in water before I sat down at the table. I was glad he loved my dress. Ken waited until I made it to the table and pulled my chair out for me before he took his seat. He is such a gentleman and a charmer.

"Thank you, Baby," I said.

"Baby Girl, you do not need to thank me for something I'm supposed to do."

I blushed a bit.

"Everything looks and smells good," he said.

"Thank you, I hope you like the food."

This was my first time cooking for him, so I was a kind of nervous. We held hands and blessed the food. He took two bites and started kissing me and saying how good the food tasted. We continued eating and talked about our day briefly.

"What are you expecting for your birthday?" Ken

asked.

"I'm not sure," I told him. "I didn't give it too much thought because with you and my girls involved, I'm sure I'll love whatever you all have planned."

"You're a good woman. You know that?"

"I know that, Baby," I teased. We laughed.

"I just want to have a wonderful time with my friends and end the evening with my man," I told him.

He said, "I'm happy you're not hard to please."

"Nope, not at all."

When we were done eating, he cleared the dinner table and I washed the dishes. Ken sipped his wine and watched me lustfully as he sat at the bar. It turned me on in a way. I knew he yearned for me sexually, but never acted on it because I wasn't giving him the right signal. I wanted so badly to strip and start masturbating right there in front of him, but I wasn't quite that bold. I don't have any sexual experience and I didn't want to look like a fool. I finished the dishes and told Ken I had to grab something out of the bedroom.

"Hurry back, Baby Girl. I'll miss you if you're gone too long."

"I won't be too long, give me a sec."

I went into my bedroom and sat on the bed. "Color, calm down. You can do this," I told myself. I took a deep breath. I was preparing myself for my next move. I never had consensual sex before, but I was curious to know what it felt like. Besides I really liked him even though I knew about his little secret. I figured I could have a few more sips of my champagne and I would be fine.

"Color, you okay in there?" Ken shouted.

"I'm fine, Baby! I'm just changing into something sexy for you. I'll be right down!"

"Shit, well in that case, take your time."

I changed into a blue corset with a matching thong and a pair of skin-colored, thigh-high panty hose. I misplaced my blue stilettos, so I settled for my multi-colored four-inch heels instead. I let my hair down, grabbed his gifts from my dresser, and headed down the stairs. Ken had the candles on the coffee table lit and soft music playing. His back was facing me, so I wrapped my arms around his waist.

"Here you go, Baby," I said excitedly.

"Color, you didn't have to get me anything. You know I prefer taking care of you."

He opened the bag and removed the tie then smelled the cologne.

"You have nice taste, Baby," he said. "I love it. Thank you."

He turned around to kiss me and noticed my ensemble. He was speechless. I stood there looking seductive, but God knew I was scared as hell. He pulled me closer into his chest and gave me a very warm hug. I took a gulp of champagne and tongue kissed him in a way that was indescribable. He picked me up and placed me on the bar. We kissed even more passionately than before.

"I love you, Baby Girl," he whispered.

"I love you back," I told him.

"Are you ready for this?" he asked me.

"It feels like I am." I replied.

I started undressing him, starting with his shirt, then his wife beater. He was so damn fine. His muscles came out of hiding, and I rubbed my hands across his firm, muscular chest before rubbing my nails across his back.

"That feels good," Ken said.

He kissed me from the front of my neck down to

my breasts. I removed my breasts from my corset so he could get a better look, feel, and taste. He untied the back of it and pulled it from around my body. Ken squeezed my breasts with his hands and licked my belly button. I unzipped his pants and they fell to the floor. I pulled his dick from his boxers and started caressing it with my hand. I felt wet. He moaned as I massaged his dick. Then he removed my hand from around his dick and licked my belly button before rubbing his nose between my thighs.

"You smell sweet," he said sliding my thong down my thighs before tossing them on the sofa. Ken kissed me again while rubbing his fingertips on my clit. It felt so good. It felt really good. My pussy started throbbing and I could feel myself getting wetter. He came closer to me and brushed his big, succulent dick against the top of my pussy then around my clit. He pushed me back on the bar and spread my legs apart and started sucking and licking my pussy lips. It was extremely intense for me. Then he stuck his tongue in my pussy hole and tongue fucked me for what felt like ten minutes straight.

"Ken, damn, Baby. Yes, ooh shit! Yeah, right there!" It was all I could say. I grabbed his ears and pushed him deeper inside of me.

"Let's make love," I told him. He looked up at me.

"You want that, Baby Girl? I can give you that. You taste so good though," he said before going back for more.

Ken lifted his head and noticed the condom I was holding. He wiped his mouth before kissing me and put the rubber on. Ken picked me up from the bar and carried me to the sofa. As he was about to put his erect dick inside of me, his phone rang. It wasn't a normal ring. It was loud and annoying. As soon as he heard it, his whole demeanor changed. Ken looked very uncomfortable and said he had to take the call. "What the fuck?" I thought. He went into the bathroom, leaving me there dripping wet to take the stupid phone call. I couldn't hear everything he said, because he'd turned the water on, but I did hear him say he'll be right there.

He came out shortly after and said he had a family emergency and had to leave right away. Ken gave me a kiss and just left. I laid there in awe. I was so horny and ready to go all the way with him, and he's gone. Just like that. No worries though, I already knew what was up.

Last week I received an anonymous text saying that Kenneth wasn't the person I thought he was. As I read the text, I thought damn, just when I start trusting his ass. It read: *Color, I know you and Kenneth have been seeing each other for months now, but there are a few things you apparently are unaware of. If you're interested in further detail about his situation, check your email.*" Immediately I became slightly upset, but more so curious, not because of what the text said, but because this person knew about me. I didn't have the slightest idea she even existed. I happened to be near a computer at the time so I checked my email and there it was, a message from Kenlady4ever@aol.com. The username said it all. I opened the message, which read:

If you're reading this email, hopefully you have already read the text I sent you. My name is Londa and I'm Kenneth's fiancé and the mother of his children. Yes, you have read it correctly. I'm his soon to be wife and we have a 3yr old son named Kenneth Jr., and I'm pregnant with our daughter Kenlon who is due next week. Kenneth and I have been together off and on for nine years. I discovered this fling between the two of you three days ago after reading through his text messages. It was obvious you had no clue about me or our kids. I also saw the picture you sent him. I must say, you are a very beautiful girl, and Kenneth is a very peculiar man. He's charming, handsome, and wealthy which is every woman's dream. I used to think he was all mine until I learned that every year he gets a younger girl, spoils her, fucks her, and breaks her little heart. I'm warning you ahead of time. He doesn't really want you. He's using you. He's in love with me and he wants his family to be together. He's obsessed with the attention and being capable of running things with his younger women. Get what you can from him now, because in a few months, he will be moving on to the next more attractive, much younger, girl. You may ask yourself why I'm volunteering this information. Well, I asked myself the same thing. "What's so different about this girl," and I figured it out. You remind me of myself. You're not in it just for the money. I can tell you really adore him, but I wish someone forewarned me before I got hooked up in all his bullshit. I could have juiced him out of everything, but I love him for who he is, not for what he has and what he can do for me. Yet, he meets all these naïve girls and lead them to think it's more than what it could ever be, they realize he won't be faithful and they cause lots of drama behind him. I have had threatening phone calls, his car has been keyed, car windows busted, and tires flattened. One of his townhouses was even set on fire and someone put sugar down his last car's gas tank. You name it, it has been done. He very well deserved it all, but I should not have had to suffer in the midst of it all. Don't get me wrong, he loves me and he won't ever leave me and I'm sure not leaving him. But this is never going to end until someone gets hurt. If you have any questions feel free to email or call me at the home number during the day.

All I could say was WOW! I didn't know whether to believe her or not, but then I noticed the family photos attached to the email. There they were, one big happy family. She was a tall, thin, dark haired White woman. Kenneth Jr. looked just like his father. There was no denying that. I decided not to bring it to his attention because I was curious to see how he was going to handle things between us. He never gave me any reason to believe he had children or another woman. Nonetheless, it bothered me because if he could hide them, what else could he possibly be keeping from me. I trusted Ken and admired him because I thought of him as being a genuine friend, but after all he is a man. Besides, I needed to feel him. He was giving me everything else I needed. I figured why not get some good sex in the process. Just like Londa suggested, I decided to milk him while he was around, at least until after my birthday.

Ken contacted me shortly after his quick escape and said he had something real important to tell me. I wondered what it could be. Could he be coming clean about his secret life? I asked him if he wanted to discuss it over the phone and he refused.

"No, Baby. I want to see you. Let's meet someplace and talk."

"I'm not sure if that's such a good idea with the way you left me earlier tonight," I told him.

"I know, Baby, but that's part of what I need to talk to you about," he replied.

"Oh really?" I asked him. "Is it something I need to hear or something you just want to tell me?"

"Honestly, it's both," he replied. "It can destroy us or help us." He suggested we meet at the coffee shop on the corner of West 3rd Street in an hour. I agreed.

In a way I wanted to hear the truth from him, but he still lied to me. When I got there, Ken was sitting at a table.

"So what's going on?" I asked him in a nonchalant way.

"I can't get a kiss before we start talking?" he asked.

"No, Ken, you can't. Look, what is this all about?"

He looked me in my eyes and turned away. I knew something was on his mind.

"You love me right, Color?"

"Yes, Ken, I do."

"Color, I love you a whole lot."

"See, now you're starting to stray away from what we're here for," I told him.

"No, I'm getting to the point." He grabbed my hands and looked me in my eyes again.

"What is it, damn?" I yelled out of aggravation.

"There's someone else."

I pulled my hands from his. "What do you mean there's someone else?" I asked playing along.

"She's the mother of my children, but I'm not in love with her."

"Children?"

"What children?" I asked. "Well, let me start over."

"Start over my ass, continue with your last statement," I said.

"We have been together for several years off and on and we have two kids together."

"How long is several years?" I asked him. "And how old are the kids?"

"About nine years. Our son is three and our daughter was born about two hours ago."

"Wow, Ken. You are a trip, dude. I can't believe this shit. How can you lie about your kids? Drama, drama, and more drama."

"Say something else, Color. I realize it's drama on my behalf, but how does that make you feel?"

"You do not want to know how I feel right now, Ken."

"I do, Baby Girl. Talk to me. I want to know what you're feeling."

"First, I want to know what the hell you want with me and why are you not at the hospital with your newborn daughter?"

"I want you," he responded. "When you and I first met, Phalonda and I were not together and like I said, I'm not in love with her."

"So, are the two of you together now?" I asked.

"No, we're not, but I love my kids and to be a part of their lives, I have to do certain things for her."

"Such as?"

"Financial things, mostly. Other times, it's just stay over some nights." he said nervously.

"Almost like an acting husband, am I right?"

"Yea, something like that."

"It's cool," I told him.

"Huh, what do you mean? You're not going to hit me or curse me out?" he asked surprised.

"No Ken, none of that. It's fine. We all have our secrets or things we don't care to discuss at first." I looked down at my watch and noticed it was five minutes after midnight. It was officially my birthday.

"Let's go in the restroom."

"Are you sure?" he asked shockingly.

"I'm sure," I said. I figured he would tell me everything, but with me already knowing about it, it didn't phase me one bit. It was raining when I left the house so I wore a trench coat with nothing underneath. Little did he know, he was in for a big surprise himself. When we got in the restroom, I pushed him in the handicap stall.

"Baby, why are you pushing me like you mad or something?" he asked.

"Shut up. I'm not upset. I'm just real hot and horny for you, Baby. You left my pussy dripping wet. Remember?"

He sat on the commode while I untied my coat. Before I could drop it to the floor, he had an erection.

"Damn, Baby, you are flawless."

"I know," I said seductively. "Let's play a little game.

"What kind of game?" he asked.

"You'll be the daddy and I'll be the mommy.

"Yea, I like that game," he commented.

I unzipped his pants, pulled his dick out, and gently caressed it. He moaned instantaneously.

"Baby, what are you doing to me?" he asked.

"I'm doing what you've always wanted me to do to you, Baby." I put his dick in my mouth and swallowed it whole. First, in circular motions, then up and down. The only sound was the sucking noises my mouth made. Smut, Smut, Smut, Slurp. It actually wasn't as bad as I imagined. I knew he would enjoy it. Then I put my heel on the toilet paper holder so he could get a closer look at my Kitty Kat. I was moister than before. I put my leg down and grabbed the handcuffs from the pocket of my trench coat.

"Baby, I don't do handcuffs," he said.

"Shhhh I got this."

I cuffed his right hand to the rail and stuck his fingers from his left hand in my pussy to feel how wet I was.

"You feel so fucking good." Then I sat on his dick. It hurt a little, but it felt better once it was all the way in.

"Ooh, Baby," I moaned. Who's dick is it?"

"Yours, Color."

I rode him slowly at first then after a few slow hard strokes, I started riding him faster.

I whispered in his ear softly, "Is it mine or Phalonda's?" I knew he felt uncomfortable, but I didn't care. He was still turned on.

"It's all yours, Color, I promise. I strangled his dick with the strength of my pussy muscles.

"It's all yours, Baby Girl." I turned around on his dick so he could get a nice view of my fat ass from behind.

"I can get use to this," he whispered. "Shit! I'm about to nut," he said.

"Are you about to cum for me, Daddy?" I asked.

"Uhn huh, I'm about to cum in that fat pussy," he screamed.

"Is this pussy the wettest you ever had?" I teased.

"Yes, I'm about to nut!"

"That's too bad." I hopped off his dick before he could cum.

"Aww shit! What you did that for, Baby? I love you and only you."

"I love you too, Baby," I told him.

"Why you gon' leave me hanging like that?" Ken asked.

"In fact, I'm going to leave you here cuffed to the railing. If you get out, the plans we made for today are still on. If you can't, have a nice life."

I laughed as I put my coat on and walked out.

"Color, wait! I'm sorry!"

"I'll see you around, Ken."

CHAPTER 7
My 18th Birthday

Later on that morning, I received ten dozen red roses and eight dozen white tulips from Ken. The card that was attached to the first delivery read: *Baby Girl, today is your special day, and I will see to it that you get everything you have ever wished for and more. Happy Birthday, Color. I Love You, Ken."* Wow, the man never stops. I was floored because no one had ever done anything like that for me. Twenty minutes after the flowers arrived, a caterer from *Campanile* delivered food to my door. Ken sent over everything on their breakfast menu. There were pancakes, waffles, ham, bacon, sausage, turkey, toast, eggs, grits, hash browns, pastries, fruit, coffee, orange juice, and milk. I couldn't eat everything all by myself so I invited Fallon and Monica over for breakfast. They were surprised and impressed when they saw the flowers and all the food he sent over.

"Girl, Kenneth is just out doing himself," Mo said.

"Yes, he is, but he's also in the doghouse," I told them.

"What? Why girl? What happened?" Fal asked.

"It's a long story. He has two kids and he's involved with their mother, as he calls it, off and on."

"Dang girl, he is in the doghouse. I'm surprised you kept him around this long. You let 'em go easily if they're dishonest," Fal acknowledged.

"It's just that I like him a lot and I know he can help me out with some things," I replied.

"Hell yea like wining and dining, helping out with some of the bills, and not to mention sex," Mo said.

"Mo, Color ain't sleeping with nobody."

"Uh, about that," I said.

"You slept with him and didn't tell us?" Fal asked.

"Damn, Fal. It just happened last night. You didn't give me a chance to tell you."

"So tell us more. How was it?" Mo asked.

"It was just sex. It wasn't romantic or anything. I just put him in his place and made sure he was aware of my good Kitty Kat." We all started laughing.

"I knew you gave him something because he put out a lot of money for all these flowers and this extravagant breakfast," Mo said smiling.

Suddenly, I got a text message. It was a text from Ken saying: *Happy Birthday, Baby Girl. I hope you're not still mad at me. P.S., Enjoy your breakfast.* I replied saying, *Thank you Ken, I'm looking forward to the rest of the evening.*

When we finished eating, I asked the girls to come with me to the mall to find a sexy outfit for tonight. Before I could finish, Mo gave me a 'Happy Birthday' bag with two boxes in it.

"Ken took care of that too," she said to me.

"Well, we helped him out so don't be afraid to open it." Fal said.

I started blushing before I saw what was inside. In the first box, there was a pair of rainbow snake skin heels with a matching clutch by Jimmy Choo. They were the baddest shoes I'd ever seen.

"Dang, Color those are very nice," Mo said.

"We didn't know about the shoes girl!" Fal revealed.

When I opened the other box, I saw fuchsia. It was a fuchsia tube-top bubble dress. It was so nice.

"Happy Birthday, girl!" Fal said.

"This man is definitely a keeper. You two really need to work things out." Mo suggested.

"All these things are nice, but money won't buy me happiness if he's laid up with the next bitch from time to time," I told them and they agreed.

"I plan on having the time of my life tonight and whatever happens from there, happens," I said.

Fal and Mo went home a little bit after to rest up for tonight. I decided to go to the boutique around the corner to pick out some accessories to wear along with my dress. When I made it there, the lady at the register asked if she could help me with anything.

"Yes you can. I'm celebrating my birthday tonight and I'm looking for some earrings, a necklace, and maybe a bracelet to wear with my dress," I told her.

"Is today your actual birthday?" she asked.

"Yes it is."

"Happy Birthday!" she said. "How has your morning been so far?"

"It's been wonderful." One of her coworkers overheard us talking and came from the back room.

"Hi, are you Color?" she asked.

"Yes, how did you know my name?"

"Your lovely boyfriend came in a few days ago and purchased some accessories for you. He brought in a beautiful hot pink dress with a pair of snakeskin heels."

"Really?" I asked. "May I see what he selected?"

"Well of course you can, Dear. It just so happened we had the perfect rainbow snake skin earrings trimmed in silver with the matching bangle. I'm not sure if you think you will need a necklace or not, but I think you'll love the two together."

She opened the jewelry box and she wasn't lying. The accessories matched perfectly.

"What do you think?" she asked.

"I love them!"

She put everything back in its place and I went back home to rest up. I changed back into my loungewear after I washed my hair. When I finally sat down on the couch, I started rolling my hair so my curls would last throughout the night. I sat under the dryer for an hour and a half and then I took a three-hour nap.

When I woke up, I had a text from an unknown number telling me to be ready for 9:30 pm. At that moment, I only had two hours to get dressed, apply my makeup, and do my hair. I wasn't quite sure what we were all doing and I didn't care. I just wanted to have a memorable evening. Once I got out of the shower, I took my rollers out and decided to pin some hair up and let the rest of it hang down. My curls turned out nice and the dress and shoes were so plush. Let the fun begin. I felt like a princess all classed up.

At 9:30 on the dot, I got a buzz from downstairs.

"Yes?" I asked.

"C'mon, Birthday Girl! We're waiting for you." It was Fal's loud mouth.

"Okay, give me a sec, I'll be right down." I told her. When I got downstairs, I noticed them standing in front of an all white, 10-passenger limousine. I was smiling from ear to ear. Ken had really out done himself, I said to myself.

"Surprise!" Ken set the limo up for tonight too." Mo said.

"Oh my God, it's so nice and spacious in here." I said.

"We have one other surprise," Fal informed me. She handed me a small wrapped box.

"What's this?" I asked.

"Just open it!" she yelled with excitement. I opened it and it was a silver heart-shaped necklace with a picture of the three of us in it.

"It's from both of us." Mo said.

"Thank you guys, it's so beautiful."

"Do you want to wear it now?" Mo asked.

"I would love to." Fal snapped it on for me while Mo signaled the driver to drive away. "Where to now?" I asked.

"We're on our way to pick up Erica, Kim, and Asia from Kim's place," Fal said.

Once we picked them up, our driver pulled into the Four Season's Hotel in Beverly Hills and we ate dinner at *Gardens*. It was real nice. They rented a private room and decorated it in fuchsia and turquoise, my two favorite colors. There were balloons everywhere and a super long birthday sign which read, *Happy Birthday Color Jade! Love, your girls, Fallon, Monica, Kim, Erica, and Asia.* I was very impressed.

"Aww girls, you all are too much. This is perfect. Thank you for putting this together for me." I almost started crying, but I knew I could not ruin my makeup so soon. We ordered our food, had a few glasses of wine, and talked. Our food came and we ate our dinner. The food was delicious. Just when I thought we were done, the server rolled out the birthday cake with the candles lit. When I saw it, it reminded me of two things; pretty and flashy. It was covered in chocolate and trimmed with turquoise and fuchsia icing in the shape of a corset. Everybody started singing, "Happy birthday to you, happy birthday to you, happy birthday Dear Color, happy birthday to you!"

I quickly blew out the candles and made a wish. I wished that I remained blessed with great friends and positive people in my circle. I cut the first slice and it was the bomb. It consisted of strawberry and butter cream filling.

"They're giving us about ten minutes to leave ladies. The restaurant closed an hour ago," Asia informed us.

We packed my gifts and the cake and hopped in the limo.

"Where are we off to now? I'm ready to have another drink," I told them.

Erica yelled out, "We're going to see some sexy ass half naked men!"

"Wooooo!" everybody screamed, except Fal.

"Wait, so you guys found a place?" I asked out of excitement.

"I really didn't want to go there, I wanted to go to a club," Fal stated.

Kim told her, "Hush girl, you just may have a good time."

"You wanna bet?" she asked Kim. "Half those men in there are probably gay anyway."

"Well if they are, they're going back straight once they see all of us!" Kim replied.

The strip spot was about 20 minutes from *Gardens*. We pulled into the club's parking lot that had a bright neon green sign that read *Big Flippers*.

"*Big Flippers*," Fal yelled. "You can't tell me that doesn't sound gay." We all laughed.

"Come on Fal," I told her, "you'll be fine."

We walked into the large building and the male greeters were wearing tiny black shorts with ripped wife beaters. They were both very muscular. One of the guys gave all of us V.I.P. passes and told us to follow him. He was cute, but he had more booty than all of us put together. He escorted us into an all white private room. We could see the rest of the club, but no one was able to see us because the other side of the glass was a mirror.

"Enjoy yourselves ladies. If you need anything, my name is Ron," he said before walking away.

"Ok Ron, nice to meet you." Asia replied. Another muscular guy wearing a white thong came in the room and introduced himself.

"Hello ladies, I'm QT and I will be your server for the evening. Whatever you request, it's yours."

Brother was cute. He had a baby's face and a baby's bottom. I knew this because I touched it.

"Well, she's the birthday girl so I need you to bring her the best specialty drink in the house," Kim told him.

"No problem. And what can I get the rest of you sexy ladies?" he asked.

"I'll have six shots of Patron and a pitcher of Long Island," Mo said.

"Dang Mo, you trying to get us fucked up like that?" Kim asked her.

"Hell yeah, Bitch! It's our girl's 18th Birthday. You only turn 18 once." she told her.

"It's all good then, especially since you buying," Kim said.

A few minutes later, QT brought out the Patron shots and Long Island.

"Come on girls," Erica suggested, "let's make a toast. Color, may you have the best 18th Birthday possible."

We all raised our shot glasses.

"To Color!" Everyone said in unison.

"Damn, that shit is strong!" Kim said.

"Ooh my throat is burning," I said.

"QT, let me get another round of Patron, please," Mo told him. "This time, bring some extra salt, lemon, and lime."

"No problem, Sweetheart," QT replied.

The Long Island was pretty good. It wasn't too strong or too watered down. It was just right. I felt my eyes getting weaker, my heart racing, and my pussy was pulsating. When I looked up, QT was back with the second round of shots. I was thinking, shit, what the hell did I get myself into? All of us took our second round of shots, and it was all over. We were unstoppable the rest of the night. Each of them paid for me to have a special lap dance from the five sexiest men in the club. It was fun and funny all at the same time. The first two guys danced together off of H-Towns, "Knocking Da Boots" and "Feenin" by Jodeci. I can't remember what the other three guys danced to because I was too out of it.

"Are you ready for your final surprise?" Kim asked.

"Oh no, there's more?"

All of a sudden I heard R. Kelly's, "Seems Like You're Ready" playing. This handsome brother came over in an all white, two-piece linen outfit. He was moving and singing along with R. Kelly's voice perfectly. I noticed how tall he was standing over me. He was dark with nice hair. The closer he got to me, the more familiar he looked. I looked over at my girls and they were sitting there grinning.

"Oh my God! Is that Ken?" I yelled out in awe.

It was definitely Ken. I thought he was so crazy for this. Ken removed his shirt and placed it around my chair. He smelled so good. That man there. He continued with his little performance even after he realized I'd recognized who he was. Ken pulled my chair towards him, got on one knee and picked my legs up and put them around his neck. Then he started licking my pussy through my panties.

"Don't do that now," I whispered.

"Stop it, Ken. Behave!"

I was beginning to feel uncomfortable because all eyes were on us. He kept touching me. He was turning me on and he knew it. Ken put his hands underneath my dress. Suddenly I thought of Momma. That was far from being lady like, but I couldn't help myself. "Sorry, Momma," I thought to myself. I felt horny and mad all at once. They both became one emotion. I gave him a huge kiss on the cheek and he tongue kissed me softly. I moved my hips along with the music. The more grinding I did, the more he touched me.

He moved my panties to the side and whispered in my ear, "I love it when it's wet."

Then he did the unthinkable. Surprisingly, he ate me in front of everyone in the room. The Patron shots and Long Island had taken over and I just sat there. It felt nice, but I was not used to being sexual, let alone in front of other people. I didn't remember much, but I heard a lot of cheering going on in the background. It was definitely a night to remember.

The following morning, I woke up in the *Millennium Biltmore Hotel* next to Ken. I had the worst headache ever. When I tried lifting my head off the pillow I felt nauseous. I ran into the bathroom and threw up. I heard Ken call out.

"Baby Girl, are you okay?"

"Yea, I said wiping my mouth, I am now." Ken came into the bathroom and put a wet towel on the back of my neck. "Thanks, Baby," I said.

"How did you sleep?" he asked.

"I'm not sure. The last thing I remember from last night is you eating me out."

"Oh really, nah a little more than that happened," he said.

"Like what?" I asked.

"Well, we had a little--"

Before he finished his statement, Asia walked in our room wearing a robe and carrying a bucket of ice.

"What the hell?" I said aloud.

"Oh hey girl!" she said. "Girl, we were so full of that liquor last night."

"What are you doing here, Asia?" I asked out of curiosity. And why do you have a key to our room?"

"Ken gave it to me," she said.

"Ken gave it you?" I asked. "Did you sleep here last night, too?"

"Yes, but--" she commented.

"Yes, but nothing!" I shouted. "Ken, what the fuck happened last night?" I asked him.

"It's not what you think baby!"

"What am I thinking, Ken?"

He responded by saying, "Asia and that dude Ron came to the room with us after the club."

"Oh really, then where is he now?" I asked.

"He left about 30 minutes ago," Asia said.

"This is a one bedroom suite. Where did you sleep?" I asked.

"We slept in the bed with you and Ken," she replied.

"Asia shut up!" Ken told her.

"Nah, let her talk!" I snapped. "Asia, what happened?" I asked.

"You and Ken watched me fuck the shit out of Ron's fine ass," she said.

"Are you serious? I don't remember a thing."

"That's why the legal drinking age is 21," Ken said.

"Thanks, yeah I strongly understand that now," I said.

"See, Baby. You had nothing to worry about. I took real good care of you last night," Ken said.

"Well I know that now," I lied, "but I also know people can't be trusted." Anything could have happened between the four of us and I wouldn't know. I'm not stupid, that's for sure. He was too damn nervous. Asia was going to reveal what really happened.

"Are you implying that I can't be trusted Color?" Asia asked. "I thought I was your home girl."

"You are my girl, but I can't put anything past you." I told her. "I just met you a few months ago. I don't know what your motives are," I said.

"That's a real insult," she said while picking up her things. "I thought you knew me better than that."

"I thought I did too," I told her. I realized she was lying through her teeth from her body language. "I wouldn't have thought you'd bring Ron home after only knowing him for a few hours either, but shit happens. Am

71

I right?"

"Whatever, Color," she said before walking out the room and slamming the door.

"I'm glad she's gone. Now I can spend more quality time with you," Ken said.

"Baby, what are we doing today?" I asked.

"I didn't make any plans for us to do anything in particular, Baby," he replied. "Do you have anything in mind?" he asked.

"Not really. I guess we can chill here or go back to my place and watch movies," I suggested.

"That's cool with me, Baby Girl."

"My back is killing me. What was I doing last night?" I asked.

"All the right things, Baby Girl. Come over here and lie down so I can rub your back," Ken said. "Let me get the baby oil."

I took off my shirt and lay on the king-sized bed while he gave me the best massage ever. Well, it felt like it could have been the best. It was so relaxing, I dozed off. Shortly after I closed my eyes, I heard shouting and knocking at our room door. Boom! Boom! Boom! Bam! Bam! Bam!

"Who could that be?" I asked.

"Only Asia and Ron knows we're here. Right, Baby?" I asked him.

"As far as I know," he said. Ken walked over to the door and asked, "Who is it?"

There was no answer. I stood up and slipped on my night shorts and threw on one of Ken's t-shirts. They continued to knock harder.

"Who is it?" he yelled.

"It's me Phalonda! Open this damn door!"

"What, I can't believe this shit," he stuttered. "Uh, hold on, Baby. Uh, give me a minute."

Boom! Boom! Boom! She kept knocking.

"Open the damn door, Kenneth!" she screamed.

"Color hide," he said.

"Excuse me? Hide for what?" I asked. "If there is nothing going on between you and her why should I hide?" I asked smiling.

"Open this fucking door now!" she screamed louder.

"Aww your baby's mother has a poo poo mouth," I said sarcastically.

He started pacing back and forth.

"Just open the door Ken!" I told him.

He was so nervous. He looked as if he wanted to break down and cry.

"You have got to be kidding me," I told him. He confirmed everything she informed me in the email. I walked towards the door to let her in and he grabbed my arm.

"If you open that door, it's going to get real ugly. She does not play when it gets down to us and our kids," he said.

"You should have thought about that before you told me it was nothing between the two of you," I said.

I opened the door and Phalonda stood there in her hospital gown that was peaking from underneath a black raincoat. She was holding their newborn daughter in her arms and their 3-year-old son KJ by the hand. I couldn't believe my eyes.

"You're in this nice hotel with this tramp two days after I had your baby? How could you, Kenneth?" she asked crying.

"Tramp?" I asked.

"I'm not talking to you right now, Color!" she said.

"Did this bitch just yell at me?" I asked myself aloud.

"If you ever want to see your kids again, you tell this young slut that it's over! Now!" she screamed.

The baby woke up and started crying uncontrollably. Their son just stood there as if everything was normal. I'm sure KJ was aware of his parent's constant arguing.

"Tell her it ends today!" Phalonda demanded.

"Go ahead, Ken. Tell me it ends today," I told him.

He began by saying, "I don't know what to say, I don't--"

"Fine," I said cutting him off. "I'll help you."

I took his hand, looked him in his eyes, and calmly told him, "Ken it ends now." I packed my things while they argued.

"I've been calling your phone for the last 24 hours to pick us up from the hospital and you couldn't even answer my calls?" Phalonda yelled. How dare you Kenneth!" she cried.

"Phalonda I can explain," Ken said.

I just shook my head. I gathered the rest of my things and bounced. They were still in the room going at it. When I got off the elevator and walked through the hotel's lobby, I felt sad, but I knew I deserved better and so did Phalonda and those poor kids. I will never forget the look on her face when I opened that door. I felt bad for her, but hey, she told me to get what I wanted out of his ass and that is exactly what I did.

CHAPTER 8
Change of Heart

After the hotel drama, Ken sold the restaurant and I never heard from him again. Fortunately, the new owner allowed myself and some of the original staff to continue working there. Two weeks after my birthday, I received a message on the answering machine. It was from the hospital.

"Hello Ms. Andrews, this is Dr. Skylark from Living Well Psychiatric Hospital. I'm calling in regards to your mother's release date. If you can, give me a call at your earliest convenience. Thank you."

I couldn't believe it. I was so happy and overwhelmed with joy. My mother was finally coming home. Excited, I returned the phone call immediately after I heard the message.

"Hi, my name is Color Andrews and I'm calling to speak with Dr. Skylark."

"Yes, would you mind holding?" the receptionist asked.

"Not at all," I replied.

"Thank you, one moment." Dr. Skylark answered

shortly after.

"This is Dr. Skylark speaking."

"Hi, Dr. Skylark its Color, Helen's daughter."

"Yes, hello Color. I was calling to confirm your mother's release date with you."

"Okay, so when should I expect her?" I asked.

"Your mother's release date is scheduled for tomorrow, but if you need us to push it back, I'll understand," she said.

"No. That will not be a problem. I'd be delighted to get my mother tomorrow. I'm surprised no one informed me in advance," I told her.

"I apologize for that, Color. We've been short staffed this month," she informed me.

"I understand. It's fine," I replied.

"Okay, good! I'll see you tomorrow," she said.

"See you on tomorrow," I told her.

Damn, I wanted Momma to come home, but I wasn't expecting her home this soon. I had so much to take care of. I wanted her to see how well I kept up with the place so I went grocery shopping, changed and washed the bed sheets, and cleaned the whole loft from top to bottom. Later, I marinated chicken wings for our dinner on tomorrow night.

"God, please give me the strength and understanding to care for my mother," I said as I cleaned. It had been a few months since we lived under the same roof. I wasn't sure what to expect. I wondered if she still liked the smell of fresh flowers and if chicken was still her favorite dish. Would she love me the same or would she hate me for what happened between Carlos and me? All of those things were going through my mind and it bothered me. Eventually I calmed down after thinking about the

76

obstacles I had already gotten through in my life. I decided Momma would be a breeze compared to that other mess I had to deal with.

When I arrived at Live Well Hospital, Dr. Skylark and Momma were in Momma's room.

"Hi Momma. How are you feeling today?" I asked her.

"I feel lovely, Baby," Momma replied. Come give Momma a hug," she said as she held out her arms. Momma looked so beautiful sitting in the lounge chair near the window. Her hair was so pretty and long, straightened. She was wearing a yellow sunhat with a brown and yellow sundress. Her smile seemed very familiar so that assured me everything was better than I expected it to be.

"It's nice to see you again, Color."

"It's good to see you as well, Dr. Skylark."

"She was just asking about you," Dr. Skylark mentioned.

"Are you ready to go home?" I asked her.

"I thought you'd never ask," Momma responded.

Dr. Skylark interrupted, "These are some sample meds, but her prescriptions are in her bag."

"Okay, thank you all for taking wonderful care of my mother."

"Ms. Helen was never a problem around here," Dr. Skylark replied. "Take care, Ms. Helen. We sure are going to miss you," she told Momma.

"That's very nice of you, Free, but I won't miss you all as much," Momma said.

"Free?" I asked.

"Yes, it's my first name. Your mother was real persistent about knowing each other on a first name basis."

"That sounds just like her." We both laughed.

"It's a different name," I said.

"Color is even more different," she replied.

"True, I guess I'm so used to it, I hardly notice," I said.

"Is your named spelled like free?" I asked her.

"No, my mom spelled it F- R- E- E-H."

"That's very unique. Dr. Freeh Skylark," I said aloud.

"My maiden name is Mei, so growing up my name was Freeh Mei like 'Free Me.'

"So were you ever freed?" I asked sarcastically.

"Very funny," she replied.

"Color, can we go now, Baby? I'm hungry and I'm tired," Momma said as she yawned.

"Sure, Momma."

"Well, it was good talking to you Dr. Skylark."

"Call me Freeh," she suggested.

"Freeh, enjoy the rest of your day." Something was different about her, but she was cool. Momma had lost some weight, however, Freeh said Momma's still healthy.

We finally made it home after an hour long drive. When Momma walked inside the loft, I noticed how impressed she was.

"Wow, Color, it's as if I never left," she said softly. "Have you been keeping up with our home all by yourself?" she asked.

"Yes, Ma'am," I responded proudly.

She had tears in her eyes. Although I knew it was coming, I wasn't prepared to deal with it.

"What happened to me, Color? What happened to us? I never meant for any of this to happen to our family," she cried out. "I should have listened to you when you were trying to talk to me," Momma sobbed.

78

"It's okay now, Momma. I love you and I'm happy you're feeling better," I told her.

"We still have each other and that's good enough," I reminded her.

We ate dinner and I put her in the bed shortly after. I changed out all of the bedroom furniture in both of our rooms. I didn't want anything reminding me of Carlos and I certainly didn't want to upset Momma.

During the middle of the night, around 3:00 am, I went into Momma's bedroom to check on her and she was sound asleep. I noticed the sheets and curtains had been thrown on the floor. She lay in bed with only her bathrobe covering her body. Apparently, Momma ripped down the window treatments and cut the bed sheets. I reckoned she had to cope with the pain somehow. The following morning I woke up to the smell of Momma's homemade buttermilk biscuits, turkey bacon, and scrambled eggs.

"I got my momma back, ya'll."

"Good morning, Baby."

"Good morning, Momma. How'd you sleep last night?" I asked her.

"I slept well, Baby, how about you?" she asked.

"I slept okay. I was concerned about you."

"Aww, don't worry about me, I'm fine," she replied. "I need to start searching for a job and work on getting my life back in order," Momma said in a worried tone.

"I knew you would be concerned about work so I did some research and made a few calls to your last job and your old position is still available."

"What did you tell them? Do they know what happened?" she asked.

"Do not worry, Momma. They know about Carlos

and they support you. However, I told them you went back to Louisiana for a few months to take care of important family matters. I told them you were so overwhelmed by the death and convictions of Carlos, that you completely didn't think of putting in a two weeks notice. They were totally accepting and empathetic to our situation. They're only aware of what was on the news and in the newspapers."

"Which is what?" she asked.

"Just that the body of convicted felon Carlos Evans was found in an alley beaten and tortured to death. It went into saying how he served time in a Las Vegas prison for the rape of his ex- girlfriend's 14 year old daughter, and that the Los Angeles Police Department, does not have any lead suspects. It doesn't mention anything about him hurting me."

She responded by saying, "Wow, I'm so grateful."

"So all you need to do at this point is speak with Human Resources on Monday morning and you're back in."

"Your father and I taught you well. I'm so proud of you," she said.

"By the grace of God, we will get past this."

"Yes we will, Momma. He forgives us and I forgive you."

We hugged each other real tight and I kissed her on her cheek. She took her pills and went into the bedroom to lie down. I looked up to the ceiling.

"Thank you, God."

A month later it felt like everything was back to normal. Momma was doing what she loved best, which was handling business. I was still working part time at the restaurant, but I missed Ken a whole lot. I enrolled in online classes with Allied Real Estate School to keep myself occupied. I wasn't a big fan of real estate, but I knew I could complete the program in about six to eight weeks and pass the exam within that timeframe. My heart was fashion. I wasn't sure what or how I wanted to pursue my fashion career. Instead of wasting time thinking about my next move, I decided to pursue the next best thing, which at the time was real estate. I was just following the money. Daddy used to always say he'd rest when he's dead. He loved us, but he loved making money. I knew he would want me to do something positive with my life as well. I felt him with us in spirit more now than ever before. Momma and I were both happy most of the time.

"I checked the messages on our answering machine yesterday and Freeh left a message saying she wants you to give her a call," Momma said.

"Okay," I told her, but I wondered what she wanted. "Thanks Momma, I will give her a call when I'm done with my home work."

I returned Freeh's call later on that evening. She asked about Momma's progression and wanted to know if I would be interested in hitting up a party on Friday night at this new club a good friend of hers had recently opened. "Why not," I thought. I hadn't been out since my birthday. I wondered if I should go alone or if I should invite Fal and Mo along too. I knew Freeh was married, but I wasn't sure if her husband would be out with her or if he allowed her to have a girl's night out once in a while.

Freeh was mixed with Chinese, Black, and White. Her mother is of Chinese heritage and her father is African American and Caucasian. She was darker than most Asian women with a petite frame. She had to be in her late twenties or early thirties, but she looked my age. I called

Fal and Mo to invite them out with me, but neither of them were available. Fal had to baby-sit her little brothers and Mo was working. I was born alone, so I definitely did not have a problem going out alone. It took me about an hour to get dressed and thirty minutes to get to my destination. I called a cab because it was always a headache parking downtown.

As I approached the door, I saw the sign, which read, *In Tune: a place to explore your every fantasy.* "What did I get myself into," I wondered. When I stepped through the entrance of the lobby, I noticed the dimmed blue lights throughout the bar area. It was even larger than I thought it might be.

The club was laid. There were white sofas, white floors, white drapes, and white tables; anything you can think of, it was white. There was different color lighting in the seating and dance areas. The music was soft and sweet. I wish my girls were here for this. On the left and right side, the seating area had purple lights and the dance floor, which was one level down from the seating area, was lit up in red. The people were sitting around mingling and sipping champagne. As I walked to my right to sit in an unoccupied chair, a server asked if I wanted any champagne.

"Sure, thank you," I told him. I took the glass, sipped on it, and sat down. While I sat there and looked around me, I noticed there were a lot more couples and single ladies than there were single men. I looked to my right and noticed the restroom sign. I finished my drink and sat the glass on the side table next to my seat. I stood up to walk to the restroom and I felt a little dizzy. I knew I wasn't that tipsy off of one drink. I wondered what was in it. When I walked down the hall towards the restroom, I was caught off guard by naked bodies roaming the hallway. As I walked down the hallway I noticed small rooms on both sides of the hall that were separated by black and red sheer drapes. Each room was lit up with candles and people having sex.

"Oh my God! Is this even legal?" I said to myself.

I didn't even make it to the restroom. I quickly turned around and was about to run out of the club when I bumped into Freeh.

"Hey, Color. I'm glad you made it."

"Hi, Freeh. Yeah, but I have to run," I told her.

She took a good look at me, looked behind me, then looked back at me again.

"Girl, don't mind them. My friends and I are all upstairs in heaven," she informed me.

"Heaven?" I asked.

"Yes, as you can see we are standing in hell," Freeh said while smiling. "Come on, I'll show you around and introduce you to everyone."

"Okay," I agreed.

I followed Freeh up the baby blue lit staircase. When we got to the top of the stairs, it was just as nicely arranged as the first floor. It was pretty much the same as downstairs, but the ceiling was lit with baby blue lights that were covered with white sheers, and white candles were on every table. The dance floor was smaller and there were more servers. Freeh introduced me to her husband, Kyle, along with their other eight friends at their table. Kyle and Freeh made a cute couple. He was a short, but strong looking, blonde haired, White guy. For some reason I was more alert, friendlier, and more talkative than usual. The servers were serving drinks, pills, cocaine, and condoms. The male servers wore white boy shorts with white bowties and the female servers wore white thongs along with white pasties in the shape of a star.

"Is this a strip club?" I asked. Everyone but Freeh laughed.

"What? What's so funny?" I asked.

"Is this your first time to a club like this?" one of her friends asked.

"I've been to a strip club before, but I didn't know people could have sex openly in a club," I told them.

"That poor girl. She's so young and naïve. Honey, this is a Swinger's Club," the woman at the end of the table informed me.

"Swingers?" I asked.

Freeh pulled me to the side. "I'm sorry, Color. I thought you had been to a club like this before. I wasn't trying to make you feel awkward or anything."

"So, what is a swinger's club exactly?" I asked her.

"It's a club that allows couples to experience non-monogamous sex between other couples or single people in a social environment," Freeh said.

"So a wife or husband swap thing?" I asked.

"Something like that," she responded.

"Why would you think I'd been some place like this before Freeh?"

"No offense, Color, but you have an exotic look about yourself. You're young, attractive, and you seem pretty open- minded."

I grabbed her hand and went into the nearest restroom.

"What's wrong?" she asked me.

"It feels like I have ants all over my body."

"Huh, what do you mean?" she said.

"It doesn't hurt or anything, it just feels funny. I'm

real horny," I told her.

"You're hungry?" she asked.

"No, I'm horny."

The next thing I knew, I had shoved Freeh against the door of the stall and tongue kissed her. She didn't stop me either. She pulled me closer, ripped my fishnet panty hose, and placed her hand on my pussy. Then she stuck her middle finger inside me.

"Come here, Sexy," she moaned.

She kissed me harder and told me to follow her through this door that was inside the restroom. It was filled with coats. Freeh laid down on the floor and told me to sit on her face. With lack of expression and surprisingly, I did just that. All I could hear was her sucking on my pussy and Sade playing at a distance. I could not fathom what was going on, but it was feeling too damn good to stop now. I'd never thought about being with another woman in that way before, but all I could think about at that very moment was having an orgasm. She stuck her tongue in my pussy and pulled it out. Then she put it back in my pussy and out again. After licking all my pussy juices, she stuck her long tongue in my ass, causing me to have an orgasm out of this world. My legs were trembling and I was unable to control them to save my life. I was finally in paradise and I didn't even realize it.

"I want more of you," Freeh said.

She flipped me over, pulled up her dress, and started grinding her shaved pussy on mine. It was weird, almost too weird to relax, but she loved it. My pussy bone was beginning to hurt.

She kissed my neck and whispered in my ear, "Your pussy's so fat," all while rubbing her clit on mine.

"Pull my hair!" she screamed. "Ooh, Color, you

Bitch! Pull my hair. Harder!"

I pulled her hair harder and she came all over me.

We were breathing heavy and before she caught her breath, she asked, "Did you like the way my pussy felt?"

"I mean, it was okay. It felt good at one point, but it's a pussy," I told her.

She pulled me closer and instructed me to put my back against the wall. Then she came closer to me again and put her legs over my thighs while they were bent. She fingered me for a minute and got me wet again. She stuck her fingers in her own pussy and put them back inside of me.

"You feel that, Color?" she asked. "That's how moist you made me."

And moist she was. Afterwards, she put her legs underneath mine and pulled my body closer to hers. She told me to ride her the same way I would a man. This was stupid, I thought. I straddled her waist and started riding her pussy bone. She opened her legs a bit more and she hit my clit with her clit and the pleasure was overwhelming. I felt it all. Before I was able to tell her how much I loved her pussy on my pussy, we both came together. It was tremendously intense.

"Did you have anything to drink?" Freeh asked.

"Yes, a glass of champagne earlier," I told her.

"From here?" she asked.

"Yea, I got it from downstairs."

"Shit!" Freeh yelled. "No wonder you kissed me. They put ecstasy in those drinks."

I said, "Ecstasy, the drug?"

"Yes the drug!" she stressed.

"How are you feeling now? Are you okay? Let me look at you," Freeh said.

"Your eyes are rolling."

"I don't feel my eyes rolling, I'm okay," I told her.

"I'm going to get you some water. Stay here," she said.

I looked in the mirror and I did not see my eyes rolling. I was still horny and I felt like a million bucks.

"Damn, I'm sexy," I told myself as I looked at my booty through the restroom's oval shaped mirror. This is the sexiest I've ever felt. I shook my booty to the background music while rubbing my fingers through my hair. Minutes later, Freeh brought me gum and water.

"Chew this and drink this cup of water."

"I don't want that, I'm fine," I told her.

"Color, trust me. Drink the water and chew this piece of gum." At that moment I didn't feel like being bothered anymore. I was feeling myself too much.

"Let's go sit down," she suggested.

Before I could tell her no, she pulled me from in front of the mirror and back into the club area. Everyone was sitting around the table looking bored and ugly.

One of the ladies at the table reached over and asked, "Are you okay, Ms. Thang? I heard you had some of that lovely champagne."

"Hazel, please mind your damn business," Freeh told her.

Freeh told Kyle she was going to take me home and come back to get him since I wasn't feeling well. To my surprise, he didn't mind. They must have had an open relationship, I thought to myself. I wasn't ready to go back home, but I didn't want to be there any longer.

"So, where are you taking me, Ms. Lady?" I asked.

"I'm taking you home, Color."

"I'm not ready to go home. The party doesn't have

to be over," I said while I rubbed my fingers through her soft hair.

"Color, calm down sweetie. I need to get you home."

I stared in her eyes and asked, "Are you sure you want me to go?"

I placed my back against the passenger door of her Lexus truck and lifted my skirt. While touching myself, I asked, "Are you certain?"

Freeh appeared to be turned on by my seductive state. She rolled her eyes as she licked her lips. I moved her hair to the left side of her shoulder and passionately sucked on her neck.

"Hmm," Freeh moaned quietly. "Can I make it up to you?"

She grabbed the back of my neck and gently kissed me. Then, unexpectedly, she placed her hands on my chest, separating us.

"Color, do we have any idea what we're doing? We can't do this, Sweetheart. It's obvious we're both strongly attracted to each other, but I'm married and I'm sure you are not single."

"You're right, Freeh. My apologies."

We drove off and after a silent 30-minute ride, we pulled up to the condo.

"Thanks for the invite and the ride. It was interesting," I assured her.

She kissed me on my cheek and said, "The pleasure was all mine."

CHAPTER 9
Let's Work It Out

The following day I woke up around four in the afternoon. I'd slept damn near all day. When I got out of bed, my mother said she was worried about me because I didn't wake up for breakfast, the phone, or to use the restroom.

"Color, are you feeling okay?"

"I'm fine, Momma. I had a long night."

"How was the party? Did you meet any friends?"

"Somewhat, but overall it was nice."

"Well, Freeh called to check on you. She said you weren't feeling well last night."

"It was a false alarm. I thought I was getting my period. It was only gas."

"Okay, Baby. Well, return her call and let her know you appreciate her for checking up on you."

"Sure, Momma, I will."

Why should she want me to return her call? She was married. What the hell am I saying? Did I really like her in that way? There was a sexual connection between us, but damn I love men. At least I think I love men. Does that mean I'm bisexual? I never even thought about being with another woman, but it was amazing. What would I say to her? I wondered. I wasn't going to mention last night unless she brought it up.

"Hello?"

"Freeh?" I asked.

"Hey, Color. Are you feeling better?"

I cleared my throat. "Uh, yeah. I'm okay. My mother said you called earlier."

"I did. I called to check on you, you know, to make sure you were okay from last night."

"Yes, I'm much better, thanks."

"Good, so would you like to hang out tonight?" she asked.

"Hang out? Hang out where?"

"It's not what you think, Sweetz. I only want us to get a chance to know each other better. It seems like you are cool to be around."

"Thank you, same to you."

"What if we have dinner? Let's say around 7:30 at the *Blue Moon.*"

"Okay sounds good, I will meet you there."

I arrived at *Blue Moon* around 7:15 p.m. I wanted to get a drink before Freeh got there, just to loosen up a bit. Only God knew how nervous I was. Where should I sit, what do I say, and more was running through my mind. Once I persuaded a cute older gentleman to buy me a Patron margarita, I sat at a two-seated table near the bar. Freeh came up behind me feathering my hair.

"You made it here kind of early I see."

"Yea, I wanted to get us a good table," I lied. I really wanted to say, "I was too embarrassed from last night to approach you at your table," but I couldn't. I hate it when I get timid about certain things. I just needed to relax and chill out.

"What are you drinking?" Freeh asked.

"It's a Patron margarita."

"Really? After revisiting the way you reacted last night, I thought you'd be drinking a Shirley Temple instead," she said sarcastically. I laughed at her statement.

"Freeh, you are so cute, but not so funny."

"So are you," she said, "I mean the cute and funny."

I giggled under my breath, realizing she was just as uptight as me. After a few more laughs and about three more drinks, we were good for the rest of the evening.

"So, what do you say you and me go work out tomorrow afternoon?" Freeh asked.

"What time in the afternoon?" I said.

"Is 3:30 okay?" she asked.

"I can do that."

We said goodnight and went our separate ways. The next day, I met Freeh at *Health & Fitness*. I wore my pink and gray jogging suit and Freeh wore black tights with a black sports bra. She was obviously in shape, carrying a six pack, and a very noticeable firm butt.

"Dang, Freeh, I wasn't aware of how fit you were."

"At my age, and with the stress of work, staying in shape is essential. Besides, it keeps me sane," she said smiling. We both laughed.

"Seriously," I said, "What's your workout regimen?"

"Cardio is my primary workout. I jog for an hour every morning, six days a week. If I happen to miss a day, I make up for it the following day. I eat dinner before 7:30 p.m. and I don't touch carbohydrates after three in the afternoon."

"Wow, I want to look nice and all, but I'm not that disciplined. I love food way too much."

"Once you get the routine going it is simple, but enough chit chatting, let's get to work."

We stretched before getting on the elliptical machine. Then we spent an hour on the treadmill, did 200 crunches, 10 sets of squats, and lifted a few weights. I expected my body to ache in the morning. When we were done, Freeh suggested we get into the sauna to relax our muscles before taking a shower. We took off all of our clothes and wrapped towels around our bodies. The sauna was both relaxing and hot. We were the only two in there. Freeh sat across from me on the side away from the sauna's entrance.

"Did you enjoy the workout?" Freeh asked.

"It was challenging," I told her. She grinned. I put my head back and closed my eyes.

"What do you think about this?" she asked.

"What?" I asked, lifting my head. When I opened my eyes, she was sitting there in front of me butt naked with her legs spread wide open. I damn near choked on my saliva.

"It's uh, I think, I ohm," I stuttered while trying to my find words.

"Shhh come here," she said softly, as we stared into each other's eyes.

I paused for a second then I slowly stood up and walked over to her and dropped my towel to the humid floor. Standing there in front of her, I looked down into her mysterious brown eyes. Freeh looked back into mine and rubbed the sweat off my left nipple before moving her hand down my chest. Passing my belly button, she headed straight for my pussy.

"Your pussy is so smooth," she whispered. She sucked both her index and middle fingers before inserting them inside of me. I moved closer to her and kissed her chin. She pushed me away as she stood up shoving me on the bench. Our pussies touched as she climbed on top of me, uniting our soft bodies as one. Moans grew louder as our clits met in bliss. There was an ecstasy of rage as we pulled hair and bit each other's nipples. Cum and sweat were everywhere. The pleasurable moment was so intense. I screamed so loud, other members of the gym called out for help.

"It sounds like someone is in trouble," I heard someone outside the sauna say.

"I heard it, too," another voice said.

I was in trouble alright. I'd been turned the fuck out and loved every second of each minute and every minute of that hour.

I asked Freeh why she decided to continue with our little love affair after rejecting me before. She said initially she and her husband wanted to partake in a threesome with me, but after the episode at the club, she could not stop thinking about me, and wanted me all to herself. Selfish right, but how could I blame her? Our eight months of lust and soon to be love and disaster, ended on the morning her husband walked in on us making love on their chaise lounge next to the bay window in their bedroom. From his reaction, I knew that he was totally uncomfortable with the fact that his wife's face was all in my ass. Not a good look for her.

"What the fuck is going on here?" Kyle yelled when he entered the bedroom.

We had been having sex since he left for work at

eight that morning. Our blended pussy juices were the aroma that filled the air. Freeh wiped her mouth on her negligee and turned around in shock.

"Kyle, Honey, I wasn't expecting you home so soon," Freeh said.

He walked up behind her and snatched her from her knees.

"You sneaky, Bitch!" he said. "How dare you do this in our house. I can't stand to even look at you," he yelled before slapping her.

I pulled my dress down and grabbed my things.

"Freeh, are you okay?" I asked trying to console her.

"Yes, go." she said holding her face and crying.

"Get out!" Kyle yelled at me. "Get out you nasty, Bitch!" he said while pulling me by my hair.

"Who the fuck do you think you are?" I screamed at him. "Don't fucking touch me. It's not my fault she enjoys fucking me and not you," I said confidently.

Kyle raised his hand to hit me and before he could touch me, I kicked him in his nuts.

"Ooh, I'm going to fuck you up, Color!" he yelled as I ran out the front door.

Our affair was very fulfilling. She taught me so much. Freeh took care of me like I was her sister, but fucked me like I was her wife for life. It was almost like no one else existed and like she had nothing to lose, but she did. She could have lost her marriage, her friends, and me as a good friend. I was content with the outcome, but I missed her crazy spirit at times. We really had a good time when we hung out. However, realistically our relationship could not be more than what it was, a few months of ecstasy. Last I heard, Freeh and her husband moved away to Atlanta, GA to be closer to his family, but if Freeh liked women as much as she liked me, it wouldn't be long before she was back in paradise with another woman.

Meanwhile, Momma had been dating this guy named John whom she met a month or two after Freeh and I were spending so much time together. Mr. John was a much older man. He took good care of my mother and he treated her like a woman deserved to be treated. Mr. John was pretty nice to me, too, but I kept my distance.

He was a successful lawyer who owned a law firm, three homes, and a coffee shop downtown. Mr. John was definitely a go- getter and he liked having extravagant things. It was his sincerity and sweet side that proved he was a great person. Mr. John was old school. He liked opening doors and pulling out chairs for ladies. He began sending my mother flowers every Monday to remind her that if she got stressed throughout the week, she had a friend in him to lean on or guide her in the right path. He sounded like a winner to me. He and Momma were looking for a home to purchase together. I thought it was too soon for that, but I felt in my heart she was happy and that he was a real genuine guy.

Around that time, I was accepted to Southern University A&M College in Baton Rouge, LA for fashion design. I had to get away from California. I felt empty there. There was so much I had gone through while I was there. I needed a change to progress in life.

CHAPTER 10
My First Home

I have been living in Louisiana for quite some time now. Campus life was convenient, but I needed my own place. It wasn't fun having to clean after other females or to find that something of mine had been eaten or taken without my approval. I decided after living on campus for three years and a few months that it was time to move into my own place.

The search for homes and condos that were the right fit for my personality and style was a challenge. I considered moving to New York after graduation and planned on renting my new home out to a small family, maybe even a college student once I moved away. I had been saving for my own place for quite a while. Most of the savings came from dancing. This was the time to do something for me. I'd been going to class faithfully and staying out of trouble for the most part, and it was time to start achieving more than just new pole tricks.

After viewing so many condos and ranch style homes, finally I found the perfect place. My name was written all over it. The home was cozy, convenient, and set at a great price. Wendy, my real estate agent, told me I would love it. Even though I knew I would more than likely be moving away within a year, I imagined it wouldn't be hard to find a buyer if I decided to sell or rent it.

Wendy and I decided to meet that morning at the first home. It was eight in the morning when she called reminding me of our meeting for eleven. I was excited.

"Good morning!"

"Good morning, Wendy."

"I was calling to make sure you were awake and ready to look at your future home," she said excitedly.

"I'm ready. I could not sleep. I was anticipating today."

"I know you are worried and quite anxious about everything, but you will be satisfied with what I have selected," she said.

"I'm aware of our similar tastes, Wendy. Nervousness is trying to take over."

"I understand. Well get yourself some breakfast and I will see you at eleven."

"Okay, Wendy, see you then."

As I pulled up to the first home, I noticed it was smaller than I imagined. The place was a cute, one bed, one bath town home. It would have been fitting for any other college student, but not for me.

"Wendy, I think it's really nice, but not quite move-in ready. The closets are very small, and there are too many windows."

"It does need some work" she commented.

"Yes, and I'm not in love with it to take on the job."

"No problem, I have two more to show you. The next place is the three bedroom, two bath house you've been dying to see," Wendy said.

"Okay, I'm crossing my fingers," I told her. Butterflies were in my stomach at that point. The first location was nice, but a little disappointing.

We drove up to this beautiful white house trimmed in gray with black shutters. Space was not an issue here. The front and back yards were very huge. I felt like turning cart wheels in the grass just like I did as a kid.

"Wow, I love it!"

"Wait a minute, Color," Wendy said. "You haven't even seen the inside yet."

We entered through the back entrance and I almost lost my breath. It was the same floor plan as my childhood home. It wasn't exactly my dream home, but it had potential. The home was located near a park, great schools, and the surrounding areas offered a variety of shopping centers and restaurants. The place had a full kitchen, dining room, and a nice size living room. There was a large patio in the back that didn't need any work. All of the signs were saying make the purchase, but before I was able to make an offer, someone purchased it. Fate had taken over, and I was forced to see other places.

Three weeks later, I moved in a two bedroom, two bath condo that was even closer to school than the home. At least I did not have to bother with the maintenance of the home or the yard. My final decision cut down a lot of costs. I painted a few rooms and cleaned the carpet before I completely moved in. One of the bedrooms was transformed into an office. Using a soft blue hue as the wall color was a wonderful idea. It made a great atmosphere to work in. I purchased white book shelves and a large white desk to finish off the office. The guest bathroom's décor was soft and simple with lots of earth tones.

My bedroom's accent wall was painted lavender. White sheer curtains hung from my window and the entrance to my balcony. A white down comforter covered my black king sized bed along with lavender and black throw pillows. Adding a large floor mirror, candles, and a chaise lounge in my spacious room created a romantic ambience. Even though the balcony was right outside my bedroom, I was not too enthused about decorating it at the time. The bathroom attached to my bedroom has black tile causing the décor to be more dramatic than the guest's restroom. Turquoise and gray were the two colors chosen to accent the black tile. The living room and dining room were painted Tibetan, an orange-red color. I did not have any furniture to complete my living room, but I was in the process of purchasing it from *Eurway* within a few weeks. Modern, sleek, and sexy pieces of furniture interest me and that is exactly what I have been looking for. I picked up a few accessories such as vases, wall portraits, plenty of candles and candleholders. There is nothing better than a clean and fresh smelling home. It felt good to finally have my own spot. I could relax and walk around naked if I wanted.

I had been talking with Mo and Fal more frequently to keep them updated about my new home. Fal is actually coming to visit me next month. She told me she wanted to come down soon as I moved off campus. I was ecstatic about her coming to visit. It had been several years since we saw each other, but we all remained good friends after all this time. Fal was not happy when I told her I was moving back to Louisiana. Eventually she got over it though. I told Fal and Mo they would be the first people I invited to my crib. Going out to clubs, smoking, and just having a good time was Fal's thing. She strongly believed that "tomorrow wasn't promised." Fal grew to be a little rough, but I guess she had to be since she was the oldest of three brothers. I couldn't wait to see her.

CHAPTER 11
Lust at First Sight

I was on my way to the New Orleans airport to get Fal when it suddenly hit me. I never revealed my sexual experiences to her. I grew a little nervous.

"Whatever happens, happens," I told myself.

I was running late after taking care of a few errands before I left Baton Rouge. I cooked and made sure the condo was clean before leaving. On my way to the airport, I stopped by *Walgreens* and bought Hershey Kisses, Fal's favorite candy. It had been four years since we last saw each other and I wanted her to feel welcomed. Although we continued to keep in touch through email and sometimes by phone, I wanted to tell her I began dating females in addition to males for the past four years. I was not sure how she would react, so I acted as if my sexual preference had not changed. Besides, I preferred discussing everything in person. I was not afraid of losing her as a friend, because she was always a loyal friend. If by any chance she couldn't accept my decisions, or me, it would surprise me.

As I arrived at the airport, Fal called and asked me to pick her up from baggage claim. I decided to park in front of the Delta Airline's entrance and wait in the car until I saw her. Five minutes had gone by when a handsome, older guy tapped on my car signaling me to open my trunk. I stepped out of my car so I could greet her with a hug. I tipped the guy five dollars after he told me Fal had gone to the restroom.

"Color Jade Andrews!" I heard a familiar voice say.

I quickly turned around and there she was standing there with an all white toy poodle in her arms. Fal appeared the same, only more masculine. Her hair was in a ponytail, but I could tell it had grown longer. She was wearing a green and black Michael Jordan warm up suit with all black J's in addition to an eyebrow piercing, a labret, and a tongue ring. Shorty was studded out from top to bottom, which totally caught me off guard. I tried moving forward with conversation, but I was stunned. This was my long time friend I was suddenly attracted to.

"Color!" she yelled out. "Color!"

"Oh, I'm so sorry, Fal, give me a hug." When we hugged, I noticed a dragon tattooed on the back of her neck. "You're looking good," I told her.

"Me? Nah, you look better, Mamacita."

We stared at each other for a brief moment before continuing.

"Color, say hi to, Iceland."

"You did not tell me you had a puppy."

"That's because I don't. She belongs to you."

"Aww, you got her for me? She's beautiful."

"A beautiful puppy, for a beautiful lady," Fal said. I couldn't resist blushing.

"I remember you saying you were lonely in your new place and how badly you wanted a poodle."

"That is so sweet and thoughtful of you. I have something for you too. It's not as big or as nice of a gift, but you love them a lot."

"You got me Hershey Kisses?"

"Yep. I got you your kisses."

"Thank you. I really appreciate that," Fal said.

We got into the car and before we were off the airport's premises, Fal asked where was I taking her to party.

"Fal, you just got into town and you're ready to get into trouble already?"

"Well I thought maybe we could hit up the strip club you work at and have a few drinks."

"Oh really? Is that right? I had something else in mind," I told her.

"What if we chill at the crib with a little champagne and catch up with each other."

"Shit, hanging with me, we may do it all." I thought to myself, she is too serious.

"Okay, we will eat dinner first and then we will decide our next move from there."

"Sounds like a plan to me," Fal agreed.

About 45 minutes later, we walked in my condo and the "Welcome Fallon" banner over my entertainment system along with balloons surprised her.

"Color, you didn't have to do all this for me."

"You know how I am. I can get a little carried away, but I was excited when you told me you were coming to visit me."

"What is that I smell coming from the kitchen?" She asked. Fal walked towards the kitchen, but I stopped her before she got close to the oven.

"Not just yet. Let us get washed up and a bit more comfortable before we eat dinner," I said.

"I do need to get out of these clothes." Fal placed Iceland in her kennel and went into her bag.

"While you are washing up, I will heat the food and set the table."

"Okay thanks, Color. I love how you decorated in here. It's real modern and cozy."

"Thank you. That's the look I was going for."

"It's nice. Where is the restroom?" she asked.

"It's right through there and the towels are in the linen closet."

"Okay, I'll be done in a few minutes," Fal told me.

"Take your time." I told her. She walked into the guest bathroom and when I heard the shower running, I changed into something comfortable before setting the dinner table. I slipped on my Victoria's Secret loungewear, the usual spaghetti strap top with Capri pants. Once dressed, I warmed the food on the stovetop and put the cornbread muffins in the oven. The table setting was a red tablecloth, white plates, and silver utensils. Fal loves listening to R&B music and smoking weed after she eats. I did not have any weed since I only smoke occasionally, but I did have slow jams. I selected The Isley Brothers, Luther Vandross, Prince, and R.Kelly to play on the CD player. She started gathering her things shortly after. Before she exited the bathroom I yelled out, "I'm finishing up in the kitchen. Go ahead and have a seat at the dinner table."

She responded, "Dang, Color. All this for me?"

"Yes and there is more to come."

I prepared Fal's favorite soul food dish. Homemade sweet potatoes, cabbage, black-eyed peas, fried chicken, and cornbread were all on the menu. When I saw her sitting at the table, I observed her appearance. Fal had changed into a wife beater and basketball shorts. Her hair was braided in two cornrows, which lead me to believe she braided it in the bathroom. Fal was even more masculine than before. I guessed that was comfort for her.

I'd bought a bottle of St. Genevieve to toast to our long time friendship.

"You can open the champagne," I told her. She popped it and poured some in our glasses as I placed the hot plates down onto the table.

"Hmm, it looks good," she said.

"Go ahead and taste it."

"Okay, but I don't eat everybody's cooking."

"I know, your funny eating behind has issues with that, but you will be fine. You are going to love it. I promise." She took the first bite and from the look on her face, I knew she loved it. "I told you I could cook."

"Yeah you did. I ain't believe you though."

"You really thought I couldn't cook?"

"Yeah, I never saw you cook a day in your life back home. Besides most pretty prissy females usually can't cook."

"Are you stereotyping me?"

"No, I'm just saying that's the way it usually is."

"It's different down south. Most of us love to cook, eat, clean, and look good."

She raised her champagne glass. "To us and our crazy ass friendship."

"To us," I said. After eating like it was our last meal ever, Fal suggested we go out for a few hours to enjoy the gorgeous day.

"We got a lot of things to talk about," she said.

"I agree. We do." I was fine with getting out of the house because I would have fallen asleep after that delicious meal.

"Don't get all dressed up either, Color. I know how you like to over dress."

"Alright, I'll just throw on some jeans, a pair of cute heels, and grab a jacket."

"That's cool."

Fal slipped on blue jean shorts and a t-shirt.

"So where are you taking me? I hope it's to a beach. I miss Cali's beaches already."

"There are not any beaches here, but we can go to the levee or a lake and talk."

"Okay, that's what's up," she said. "As long as we chill by water, I'm good."

I parked on the side of the street across from the levee's entrance.

"Wow this is dope," she said.

"I come here when I feel like thinking to myself. It's so peaceful," I told her.

"It really is," she said agreeing with me. "What do you think about when you come here alone?"

"I think about things from my past and how much of an impact it has on me and the decisions I make today."

"I feel you on that. So are you having a hard time making certain decisions now or is everything in order?"

"Everything is taken care of for the most part," I responded. "I just have to let the rest happen. You know what I'm saying? I just bought the condo, I'm graduating soon, and possibly moving to New York. There is nothing stopping me now. I'm blessed and I will take advantage of whatever else God gives me." She looked at me with concern.

"You still have faith in God?" she asked.

"Of course I do, Fal. I mean, yeah I have been through a lot, but who hasn't? Life is not going to be perfect. We have to go through trials and tribulations so that we're grateful for the blessings in our lives."

"I understand," she said.

"We fall so that we can get right back up. Without mistakes and flaws, we would not learn anything. Life is really what you make of it. If people would use their God-given skills and talents, they could be overachievers."

"So, in other words, whatever your strengths are, use them?" Fal asked.

"Yes, that is exactly what I'm saying. Turn negatives into positives."

"Give an example," Fal said.

"For instance, I was blessed with money from my father's death. I invested it into a home. I got approved for partial financial aid. I danced to pay for school. I love everything about fashion. My major is fashion design and I sew. My point is that I use the tools I was blessed with to get what I want out of life. All of my positives could have easily turned negative. Such as, my body is too sexy; maybe that is why I was raped. My father died and left me money so I'm going shopping to ease the pain, or I was only approved for some of my school funding so I can not go to college. There are quite a few people out there who are always so negative and make excuses for everything that goes on in their life, but I am definitely not that person."

"Damn, Color. You had me kind of scared there getting all serious about it and stuff. I was not trying to upset you about anything," Fal said.

"I am not upset, Fal. I wanted to express my feelings in general."

"I feel everything you are saying. Only if the world could have a lot more Color Jades' running around, we would all be okay."

"We would huh?" I said jokingly. We both laughed.

"How is your tattoo shop coming along?" I asked her.

"It's fine. I am thinking about selling it though."

"What? Why?" I asked. "What do you mean you're thinking about selling it?"

"It's a whole lot of responsibility and I'm just not interested enough to run it anymore."

"Fal that is your livelihood. It's your baby. I remember when you called me and told me you bought it. You were so happy and proud of yourself for doing something for you without the help of anyone else. Are you sure you want to do that?"

"Not really. I love my job, don't get me wrong, but I would rather work in someone else's shop."

"You're kidding me, right? People pay you to do their work in your shop don't they?"

"Yes they do, but it is not much of a profit for me because most of the time, they are late paying me booth rent."

"Well, you need to fire them and get you a reliable, experienced team of tattoo artists. Maybe you should think things through before you sell it so soon."

"I have been thinking for a while now."

"How long has it been in business?" I asked.

"*Canvas Ink* has been in business for one year and seven months."

"That's it?" I asked. "According to my business

professor, businesses usually see their profit after about three years," I informed her. "Maybe you should try changing a few things in the shop. Spice it up. You can try things like selling rock and alternative music, t-shirts, and all kinds of cool body jewelry. Just be creative!"

"Those are great ideas. I will start calling around and researching this week," Fal said.

"Now that is what I like to hear," I responded. "How are your brothers and your mother doing, Fal?"

"They are all doing well. My mom told me to tell you hi and my brother PJ said what's up with you and him."

"Your little brother better go ahead with all that. His lil young butt can not handle me," I told her.

"I know. He can't, but I can," Fal said. My mouth fell open and I thought I was hearing things.

"Huh? Excuse me," I said. "What do you mean, Fal?"

"It means what I said." Before I could respond, she kissed me. Damn that girl can kiss.

"Oh my, God. What have we done? Where did that come from?" I asked embarrassed.

"It came from the heart," Fal said as we looked into each other's eyes.

"I'm flattered, but what about our friendship and your boyfriend Shawn?"

"Shawn was my girlfriend. Don't worry about her. It has been over between us for a couple of months now," she said convincingly.

"Why didn't you tell me?"

"Tell you what?" she asked me.

"Tell me you liked girls!"

"Because I don't like girls I like women."

"That's funny, but I am for real," I told her.

"Well, I thought you would look at me different," Fal said. "I value our friendship and I did not want to lose you over something I couldn't control." I laughed aloud.

"What's so funny," she asked out of curiosity.

"Me!" I said. "Us! I am trying to say, I like women too, but I wasn't sure how to tell you either," I told her.

"That is crazy," Fal said agreeing with me.

"So are we good?" I asked.

"Yeah, it's all good now. But there is one more thing I need to tell you," Fal said.

My throat got dry and I started feeling a little queasy. "What is it?" I asked.

"I have been crushing on you since we first met. When I saw you standing near Principal Lache's office with your two pigtails and you smiled at me, I was in love. I knew even at age nine the feelings I had for you weren't normal. I tried forgetting about it, but every time I saw your smile or made you laugh, it felt natural," Fal revealed.

"Wow, I'm not sure what to say," I told her.

"You don't have to say a thing," she said. "I've been waiting to kiss you all these years."

"So does that mean you were only pretending to be my friend back then?" I asked.

"Not at all, Color. Just like I stated earlier, I value our friendship. I love you as a friend."

"I love you, too, Fal. I just don't want our attraction to one another to change that."

"No matter what happens, I will always be your friend and you will always be mine. Our friendship is forever," Fal said smiling.

"Like we used to say: 'Extreme best friends for life'," I replied.

CHAPTER 12
Sexual Gratification

After leaving the levee, we headed for *Tits & Wings*. I warned Fal about the name before we even got there. She laughed. We walked in and there were people everywhere. It was college night so it was packed with lots of athletes and single women. I knew Fal was pleased the moment we stepped into the club.

"It's crowded," Fal said. "I bet you make good money in here."

"For the most part I do. I see a few of my regular clients in here too."

"Damn, you call them clients? That shit is hilarious."

"I told you, I'm a hustler."

"Yeah, whatever, Color. I'll be at the bar."

"Cool. Take your time," I told her. "I'm going to say hi to the girls in the dressing room."

"Cool," she replied. "I'll probably be getting a lap dance or at the bar throwing back shots."

"Alright. Enjoy yourself." I walked in the dressing room and saw my girl Mocha getting all oiled up by Envy.

"What's up ladies?" I said as I entered the room.

"What's going on girl?" they all said at once.

"Nothing much. I'm just showing my best friend around."

"Well if she likes pussy, you brought her to the right place," Envy said.

"We'll make sure she has a good time," Mocha added.

"Cool. I'll let her know to look out for you two."

"We about to get ready for Candy's birthday set."

"Oh, I forgot today was her birthday. Where is she?" I asked.

"Girl, somewhere out there getting wasted," Mocha said.

"I bet she is, she's 21 now," I said and laughed as Candy walked in the dressing room.

"Heeeaayyy Climaxx!" Candy said.

"Hey Birthday girl! How do feel?" I asked her.

"Like a woman!"

I pulled a $20 bill and a dollar out of my back pocket and pinned it on her top.

"Aww, that's so sweet of you," Candy said.

"It's your birthday," I told her.

"Come dance with the birthday girl then."

"I'm not working tonight."

"You don't have to be on the clock to dance," she said.

"I can dry hump you." We all started laughing at her silly drunk ass.

"Candy, what clock?" Mocha asked.

"Shit, well you bitches know what I'm trying to say."

"I'll dance a lil later for you then," I said. "Okay, honey?"

"My name ain't Honey. I'm Candy," she told me.

"That's alright. Girl you're fucked up. Just come dance for me and my best friend at our table a little later," I told her.

"Okay, but I can't promise you I'll be any good by then," Candy said.

"It's fine if you can't make it, but we will be at the second table near the bar."

"Alright Climaxx girl, I'll see you later," she said before walking out of the dressing room. I went back into the club area and Fal was still sitting at the bar. She and Diamond, one of the dancers, were taking Patron shots together.

"Color, come on and take a shot," Fal said.

"You know I only mess with lemon drops now.

"Take a lemon drop shot then," Diamond suggested.

"I hate taking shots. Every time I take shots I get sick."

"I'm about to buy you a Patron shot anyway," Fal said.

"Alright, I'll take it," I told her.

"Bartender! Give us another round of Patron!" Fal yelled.

"What's up, Honey? Hook us up girl," I said.

"I got you, Climaxx," Honey said as she sat a glass filled with lemon and lime on the counter next to the three Patron shots.

"Okay, Color. You ready?" Fal asked.

"No, wait!" I said.

"Listen, all you got to do is take the shot in your hand, put it to your mouth and hold your head back then swallow," Fal said.

"Then you take a lemon or a lime and suck on it afterwards," Honey added.

"I know how to take shots. I just prefer not to," I told them.

I took the shot and I actually liked it. The Patron didn't seem as strong as the Patron shots we took during my 18th birthday celebration. I ordered two more rounds and from there on, we got messed up. We must have spent $200 at the bar and $150 on the dancers. We got so wasted, I lost my car keys. I had to wait until everyone was gone before I found them. Fal was chillin. I knew all she needed was a fat blunt and she would be in heaven. Earlier I had gotten a half ounce of marijuana from Mocha's ol' man, the best weed in the city I heard.

On our way home I stopped by *Circle K* and bought a pack of Strawberry Phillies, two packs of BC's, and a liter of Sprite. I felt like I would have a hangover so I needed to be prepared for the worse. Finally, we made it home. I turned on the CD player and cut on the lamp next to the sofa. I told Fal I had something for her and to get comfy. She went in the back and changed clothes while I took a shower. I had placed the weed and blunts on the coffee table with a note that said, *I know this is all you need to finish off your night. Enjoy, I'm going to take a quick shower.*

Candles were lit and scented oil was burning. I hate for a house to smell like smoke so I made sure of taking care of that before I left out of the living room. I jumped in the shower and washed the smoke smell away from my hair, then I washed my body with my new shower gel fragrance Couture by Juicy Couture. It smelled so enticing. After showering, I wrapped a towel around my hair, and slipped on my red satin robe. When I walked back into the living room, Fal was lounging on the sofa. R. Kelly's greatest hits were playing on the stereo and she was smoking her blunt. I sat right next to her. She hit it twice and passed it to me. I felt relaxed, maybe a little too relaxed. Before I knew it, I was doing things I would not have done sober.

"Are you dealing with anyone?" Fal asked.

"Not at the moment," I responded. "I have friends, but nothing serious. Why do you ask?"

"I was just wondering," Fal replied.

Maybe she wanted to make sure no one would be breaking through my front door at any given moment. I sat there beside her with my heart racing and my pussy throbbing. I took a deep breath, put my legs across her thighs, and fondled through her hair.

"That feels nice," Fal said as she put her head back and closed her eyes.

It felt good to my hand, too. I grabbed her head pulling it towards me and I kissed her. Our first kiss had nothing on this one. This kiss was magnetic. I climbed on top of her straddling her lap. With both of my hands in her hair, I massaged her head while we kissed. She smelled real pleasant. The cologne she wore must have been called Dickmatized because the fragrance was calling every part of my body. Fal stood up with my legs still wrapped around her waist.

"You're all I need to finish my night," she whispered, which turned me on even more.

She carried me into my bedroom. Our kisses had

grown more fiery. As she held me up, I untied my robe. My nipples were so erect. She paused for a moment to suck on them. My pussy became moist for her within seconds. Fal pushed my unclothed back against the cold wall and slipped her fingers inside of me. We both moaned the instant she felt the inside of my pussy. Sexual gratification is all I need to say. It felt tastefully appetizing.

"Fuck! You feel better than I could have ever imagined," Fal said.

She pushed me closer into the wall then positioned herself closer to me. Then she pulled down her pants, revealing her strap. I couldn't see the color or the size of it, and it did not even matter. I only wanted to feel her love inside of me. She gently pushed it in after rubbing it against my clit, teasing me, making me yearn for it even more. My pussy was delighted to greet her dick. It was an average eight to ten inches, which was perfect for my "Strawberry Glaze." It wasn't too big or too small, it was just right.

I began grinding her, slowly and gently. Fascinated by my pussy- tightening techniques, Fal's soft moans grew intimately. The more she moaned the tighter I gripped it. That motherfucker was turning me on so much, I spanked my own ass. I was naked while she still wore her sports bra and boxers. I stripped the remaining garments from her firm body. It had been a long time since I felt such great sexual pleasures, but I attempted to lure her instead of making my lack of sexual exploitations visible. I allowed Fal to take control.

Fal fucked me doggy style for at least forty minutes. After six orgasms, I had to stop. She had taken over and I was like a kid begging for more and more. That's just what she gave me. Fal pulled me closer to her as she pulled my hair. She spoke to me in Spanish as she held my ass cheeks apart and applied pressure to my pussy.

"Ooh Fal, you can't be doing this to me," I cried out. "It's too good! It's too good to me," I screamed.

Fal slapped me on my ass and said, "Te encarta esta pija de cali eh?" I could not maintain my composure.

"Oh shit! Yeah, Baby, I do. I do love that Cali dick!" I loved it all too much. Before I knew it, the sun was rising as we both came in unison. It was the best orgasm I had all night. Afterwards, we laid in bed side by side. I remained on my stomach face down in the sheets while Fal got up to get the blunt out of the living room. She returned to lay next to me.

"Talk to me, Color. How are you feeling?" Fal asked me.

"I feel good. I'm comfortable with you," I reassured her. "How did you expect me to feel?"

"No special way," she said.

"I'm just making sure you're okay," she added.

"Thanks. I'm fine."

Fal handed me the blunt and went underneath the covers. I surrendered myself as her wet tongue slid over my clit. Clitoral pleasure was my weakness. I proceeded to hit the blunt one last time before placing it on my side table to concentrate on what she was doing. Fal devoured my essence, eating me whole. She lifted her head seconds later.

"Fuck, Mamacita, you taste too good!" Fal yelled.

Fingering me in my ass while she ate my pussy was the ultimate arousal she had provided all night. The way we communicated sexually was amazing. It was fascinating. We were both lured by each other's desires and it was the greatest escape of all time. I came again, again, and again after that. Fal lifted her head from under the covers and lay in between my thighs, kissed me softly on my neck and caressed my breasts.

"Damn, Sexy," Fal said. "You'll keep my dick hard."

CHAPTER 13
Eye Candy

Fal and I kicked it for a short while, but we never tried to pursue a relationship further than the friendship we established over 15 years ago because we were at different places in our lives. I was focused on my goals. Fal, on the other hand, was focused on partying, looking good, and fucking, which was okay. However, that shit didn't pay my bills and it sure as hell wouldn't get me where I wanted to be. Fortunately, she still has her tattoo shop, but she hasn't made any arrangements to improve the place. I will always love her as a friend, but sometimes we have those friends we can only love at a distance in order to get past hurdles in our own life.

During the first three years of college, I managed to save $15, 800.00 between dancing at the club and sewing costumes. It wasn't much, but if something came up, I'd be prepared for it. I did a little splurging here and there, but I never overdid it.

As far as my love-life, I dated a few people, here and there, but nothing too major. However, I met a stud named Emery, who goes by the alias Hush, whom I have become fond of. You can say I dated a guy named Corey, for a short while, but he was just that, a date. Corey and I met on campus. He was an average guy who had most of his priorities together, but he was looking for a wife and children, everything I was not equipped for. Hush, on the other hand, was perfect eye candy. She and I were introduced by Mocha after I gave her a lap dance. I felt Hush watching me throughout the night. I noticed her, too. I thought she was attractive, and it was obvious she was balling from the way the other dancers lined up in V.I.P. to get a dance from her. I remember it so vividly.

She was wearing Rocawear from her head down to her feet. Hush graced the club with swag from here to yonder, as we say in the South. Flossing a low hair cut, her diamond crusted grill, along with her chain, shined from across the room every time she opened her mouth. Tattoos covered her left arm in addition to the word "HUSH" and a pair of red hot lips tatted on the right side of her neck. The artwork appeared new, but maybe it was the lightness of her skin that deceived me.

I stood by the bar observing the looks on the other girls' faces as they stood in line waiting for Hush to notice them. They were all in. Most of them disliked lesbians, or dykes as they would say, but they were not being too judgmental when she pulled stacks of money from her pockets. My strategy for getting dances was simple. The client looked for me. I never asked if someone wanted a dance because I never had to. It was understood by my customers, or any potential customer of mine, to approach me or send for me if they wanted me for entertaining, which is what Hush did the night we met. She was sitting in V.I.P. with her bottle of Moet when Blossom, the club's waitress, tapped me on my shoulder and told me that Hush was interested in partying with me.

On that particular evening, I was looking extra sexy. My hair was wavy and hung down my back. The royal blue two- piece dance outfit I wore, which was covered in iridescent rhinestones, hugged my body in the right places and sparkled as I swayed throughout the room. With my five inch wrap- around rhinestone heels and my body bronzer glitter covering my entire body, I waited.

"Climaxx, that dyke over there want a dance from you," Blossom said to me. "She gave me a $50 bill just to come over here and get you. She asked me, 'Who is that over there?' I told her, 'That's my girl, Climaxx.'"

"Okay, I'll be over there when I finish my drink," I told Blossom.

"You betta' hurry Bitch. That chic is paid! She be kickin' it with Mocha's ol' man, Greg and them. These hoes been on her all night. Go on over there and make your money girl."

I took two sips of my lemon drop martini, reapplied my cherry lip gloss, and then slowly walked over to her table.

"Hey. Blossom said you wanted a dance from me."

"Yea, Ma. I want several dances from you."

"That's fine. The dances are two for $30, four for $50--" She interrupted me before I finished what I was saying.

"What about a G for the whole night?" she asked.

"Oh, I'm sorry, but I do not get down like that."

"Like what?"

"I don't sleep with my clients for money."

"Who said I wanted to fuck, Ma?"

"Usually when someone requests the whole night, they are referring to fucking," I told her.

"I'm saying though, I wouldn't mind that, but I can clearly see you deserve the utmost respect."

"Okay, I can give you that. But first, let me get this straight, you want to pay me a grand just for dancing?"

"Yea, Baby, that is all."

The only thing I could do was blush. "I'm in Love with a Stripper" was the first song that ripped through the loud speakers. I started dancing for her with my back towards her. Customers were not allowed to touch us, but Hush managed to move my hair to the front of my left shoulder then proceeded to rub her hand down the center of my back. I did not mind. It was soothing. Three songs later I realized the other dancers were staring over at us with envy. I paid them no attention. I was making money and whatever decisions I made were my very own. The sexier I moved, the more money piled up around my heels like leaves on a windy fall day.

"You so fucking sexy, Ma. You smell real good, too," Hush said.

"Thank you," I told her. Mocha and Greg came over.

"Hush," Mocha said. "I see you met my homegirl, Color, aka the infamous Climaxx."

"Something like that," Hush replied. "I'm trying to get to know her on a personal level though."

"Hush, you a trip. You know damn well your ass can't commit to just one woman," Mocha replied.

"Whatever, Mocha! Cousin, get your ol' lady man." Greg stood there and smiled.

"Baby, let my people handle business," Greg commented.

"Well enjoy the rest of your night," Mocha said. "I will see you in the dressing room later for details girl."

"Ok see you later, Mocha."

I danced for her the rest of the night and afterwards we met up at *IHOP* for breakfast. We ate, she paid, and then we went our separate ways. She called me a few times after that night, but I always missed her calls. I was either in class or working. When I tried returning her call, she never answered.

One night, unexpectedly, I received a dozen of white roses from her at my job. The card read: *Color, I hope we get up soon. Call a nigga or something. I saw these beautiful roses and thought of you. Your New Friend, HUSH.*"

I was flattered. I was not expecting anything from her. Immediately I called her to say thanks. Ironically, she answered. Later that night, she came up to the club and bought a bottle of Remy, Patron, and Moet. Four girls, including myself, danced for her and her best friend, Black, in V.I.P. to celebrate Black's Birthday. I danced for Hush, while the other three ladies danced for Black. She was nothing like Hush. They were totally opposites, but close like sisters. Black's hair was long and straight, she was dark skinned with beautiful white teeth. Her style was preppy in comparison with Hush's. She wore skinny jeans, high top All-Stars, a fitted tee, and a baby chain.

Hush, on the contrary, was just as thugged out as before, but that was who she was. She was so confident being herself. I began admiring her on that night.

Once the club closed, Hush and Black waited outside in the parking lot and talked to Mocha and Candy while I got dressed. Candy and Black were together for a couple of years before splitting up a few weeks ago. I'm assuming they still fuck every now and again.

The four of us went back to my place and had a few more drinks and played Spades. Candy and I whooped their butts. We must have been up playing for quite a while because when everyone left, daylight was peaking through the clouds. Hush asked me to have dinner with her the following evening. She picked me up at 7:00 pm and we headed to *J. Alexander's*, one of the best steakhouses in Baton Rouge. She was such a comedian at heart and she was very intelligent.

"So, Color what kind of Pisces are you?" she asked.

"I am the emotional, intuitive, romantic kind," I told her.

"You really believe in your intuition?" she asked.

"Most definitely, I do. My mind always tells me what I need to know and exactly when I need to know it."

"I need to be careful around you then huh?" she commented.

"Don't be cautious, just be mindful that I am not your average chic."

"That's what's up," she said. "That's why I like you, you're so different."

"Thank you, if that's a compliment," I said. We both laughed.

"What about you, Hush? Do you have most qualities of a typical Aries?"

"I would say I'm not as selfish as most Arians. I love hard, hustle hard, I may withhold my true feelings at times, and I love a good challenge."

"It does not sound like we will have a problem getting along," I told her.

"Nah, not at all." She continued. "Have you ever

been with a girl before?"

"Yes I have." She seemed shocked to learn that I wasn't new to this.

"Is there a problem?"

"No, Ma, no problem. Do you consider yourself bisexual?" she asked.

"Yes, but I prefer women."

"Ok, that's cool."

I asked her, "How long have you been a part of the lifestyle?"

"Man, since I can remember. I had a girlfriend when I was in the first grade."

"What? The first grade! You were only like six years old, right?"

"Yea, I was only six."

"I couldn't imagine being gay that young. I was 18 when I had my first girl on girl experience," I revealed.

"Was it with a femme girl or a stud?"

"She was a feminine woman."

"Ooh whee. I wish I could have been there to participate." We laughed.

"I bet you do," I added.

We finished our meal and swung by *The Pool Room* for drinks and a game of pool. We had a wonderful time. She mentioned Hurricane Katrina and the way it destroyed the city of New Orleans and how devastating it was for she and her family. Hush told me she lost her home on the lake along with everything else she once owned. Her mother was one of the people who decided to stay and sit it out, but unfortunately did not make it out alive. I told her how sorry I was for her loss. She began getting emotional so I quickly changed the subject.

"When was the last time you had a girlfriend?" I

asked.

"It has been over three years. The female I dated for three and a half years went back to her baby's father."

"Damn, I'm sorry to hear that," I said.

All I thought about was how much she's gone through. No wonder she was single for such a long time. She had trust issues.

"You are actually the first girl I've liked since my ex- girlfriend," Hush revealed.

"Wow, really? I'm flattered."

"It's true, Color, I want you. I want to be with you and love you in the near future."

"You hardly know me."

"Tell me what I need to know about you then. I feel as though I know enough."

"Like what?" I asked out of curiosity. "What do you know besides the obvious?"

"I know you hustle hard like me, you've had your heart broken like me, you are about your business and according to your appearance in and outside of work, you love fashion."

"Very impressive," I said. "Everything you mentioned is true. I have gotten hurt before, I'm in school for fashion design, and money does motivate me," I told her.

"Every reason for me to get to know you. We are so much alike," Hush said.

"I agree. It sounds like we have a lot in common," I said blushing.

I never asked her what kind of business she was in simply because I really did not want to know the true answer. According to Blossom, Hush was into distributing illegal drugs, something I couldn't afford to be a part of. I liked her. I just didn't want to move too fast. With school and graduation approaching, Hush would certainly be a distraction.

CHAPTER 14
He Loves Me, but I Love Her

Corey first approached me in the library on campus during the beginning of last semester. He was a pretty boy, always fresh, and dressed nice. He happened to be a fashion design major as well. We dated for a few months until I realized how overprotective he was. He never liked the fact that I was an exotic dancer. I invited him out to *Tits & Wings* a few times, but he only came once. Even then it was obvious how uncomfortable the environment made him feel. He did not drink, or smoke, and he definitely did not do strip clubs. On the flip side, Corey was romantic, sweet, and a very good listener. At times I would get uncomfortable with his over possessive ways, which started after we had sex. It was a great thing he moved back to Michigan after he graduated, because I would have had a pest on my hands. Three months of smiles with a dab of drama was enough reason for me not to fall in love and marry a guy like Corey. I was too much of my own woman. He deserved a woman who wanted to be led by the hand and submit to her man.

My mother would have adored him, but they were never able to meet, although I would love for her and Emery to meet. I wasn't sure how Momma would have reacted to me dating a female, but I assumed she would respect it. I was not raised to judge or dislike people who were different. However, I did not want to give her anything in addition to Mr. John's health situation to be concerned about.

Graduation was a month away so when she and Mr. John comes down, she would get the chance to meet her then. Hush was nervous about the idea of meeting my mother. Even after seeing each other exclusively for five months, she cringed at the thought of even being near my mother. I told her all about the situation with Carlos and my mother being sick after it all happened. She totally disagreed with the way my mother handled everything, but I let her know she had been making up for it ever since.

Hush was giving me a graduation party at the strip club next month and I couldn't wait. She wasn't too happy about me relocating to New York, but I planned on traveling back and forth. Maybe she would move up there with me. Yeah right. I love her, but Hush was in her comfort zone here. The first few months we dated were fun and exciting. We went to Houston's Gay Pride Splash and balled out of control. When we returned home, she became somewhat distant. I began receiving prank calls on my cell, home, and work phone. I informed Hush of the unwanted calls, and she swore she had nothing to do with any of it. Supposedly the isolation started because she was slipping with work and other priorities. I understood, but I missed her company so much. She had grown on me so fast. It was by far the best relationship I had ever been a part of. Hush pampered and spoiled me to death. The less she came around, the more prank calls I received. The person would call me twice a day, hold the phone, and breathe hard into the phone's receiver. It was like clockwork. I would get a phone call around 6:30 pm, which was when I got home from school and again at four in the morning, which was when I usually arrived home from working at the club. Whoever this prankster was had no idea I'd stopped dancing two months ago. One evening while Hush and I watched movies, someone painted both sides of my car. SLUT was written on the driver side and DYKE was written on the passenger side. I was heated! Luckily, Hush knew the owner of an auto body shop, so it was taken care of the following day.

Finals were coming up and I really could not deal with any extra drawbacks. It was a few weeks before graduation when things got real crazy. One rainy day, while on campus taking a final, my windshield and rear window was broken out of my car. I called Hush and she came to the rescue.

"Damn, Color! Somebody is after you."

"After me? They are trying to ruin my fucking life!"

"Calm down, Ma," she said.

"Calm down? All of my things are getting soaked; my final design project is ruined. I don't know what to do," I cried out.

"First you need to call the police and file an incident report, then you need to get an alarm for your car, and some protection," Hush suggested.

"You are right, Baby."

"What happened to you taking care of that when I told you to? Safety should always come first beautiful."

"I will take care of it as soon as possible," I replied.

I reported the incident to the campus police, who were reluctant to get involved, so I contacted the local authorities and filed a complaint. That way, if something else happened I would have already filed, and they would be familiar with my situation. We called a tow truck company to take my vehicle to the shop for repairs. It took two days for the windows to be repaired and to get my car alarm installed. I drove Hush's Range Rover to get around until my car was fixed. I appreciated everything she was doing and had already done, so I planned to do something special for her in return.

It was on a Saturday, the perfect time to surprise her, when I picked up my vehicle. I prepared a nice romantic candlelit dinner at my place for my Hushy- Pooh. I set white candles throughout the living room, dining room, bathroom, bedroom, and balcony. Blue rose petals lead from the front door to the balcony where dinner was being served. White lace and sheer curtains were draped and hung off the balcony. I placed a single white rose in the vase on the dinner table.

My car was around the block so when she picked me up to take me to get my car, I'd already lit all the candles. I planned it all out. She would walk into the apartment filled with the smell of shrimp pasta, and the aroma of magnolia scented candles. I was going to give her a special lap dance after dinner. Janet Jackson's Velvet Rope played in my CD player.

I heard Hush toot the horn after I lit the last candle. "She is right on time," I thought to myself. I closed the door behind me and locked it. Less than fifteen minutes, we were back at my place. When I unlocked the door, every room was pitch black. There was not a single candle lit. Immediately I panicked.

"What's wrong, Ma?" Hush asked. I cut the light switch on and noticed the white rose had been moved from the balcony to the living room's floor and set a fire.

"Someone was in here! They are truly stalking me," I told her. "Before I left, I lit all of these candles and now they are all blown out, and that rose was not burned."

"Baby, are you sure?"

"Yes I'm sure. I'm not going crazy Hush, I know how I left my stuff."

"It doesn't seem like anything was touched." Hush said.

"It doesn't, and that is the scary part." I started crying.

"I just don't know what to do anymore. It is way too much for me to deal with right now." I checked on Iceland and brought her in the living room. Oddly she would not stop barking; even when I picked her up into my arms. I put her down and closed my blinds. We checked the condo thoroughly, but everything else was in its proper place.

"Color, just come to my place tonight."

"I'm scared to leave my things," I said.

"Besides, we should call the police before we go anywhere."

"Well it is late, and nothing was stolen so they may think you are out of it."

"I don't give a care what they think. I live alone and I can not be dealing with all of these issues two weeks before graduation, especially since I have not even started redoing my final design project yet."

"Okay, Baby, we will call the police."

"911 what's your emergency?"

"Uh yeah, I'm at a friend's apartment and someone just broke in."

"Is anyone hurt?"

"No."

"What's the address?"

"548 Palmetto Lane NW 75024 is the zip."

"I'm sending someone out there now."

"Thank you," Hush replied. We waited outside in my car until Officer P. Thurman and Officer Mayweather arrived. I gave my statement outside and then all of us went into the apartment to search it.

"What the hell?" Hush yelled out.

"What?" I asked. I walked in and my place had been trashed.

"They were here all along," Officer Thurman said.

Someone had broken my glass dining room table, my glass coffee and side tables, spray painted my pictures, broken some of my dishes, ripped down my living room and bedroom curtains, and crashed my 32' plasma television. Officer Thurman asked if I had anyplace to stay the night. I could not bring myself to release any words. I was completely speechless. All I could do was sit on my sofa and cry.

"Who would do this? What am I suppose to do? Who's going to clean this mess up?" I yelled.

"Baby try and take a deep breath and calm down."

"What's your name?" Officer Thurman asked Hush.

"I'm Emery."

"How do you know this young lady?"

"We are good friends," Hush replied.

"How long have you two known each other?" he asked.

133

"Wait what does she have to do with someone breaking into my place," I interrupted.

"It's just procedure, Ma'am."

"Procedure? I live here all by myself. Imma' need you to proceed to the next step and find the person who did this."

"Ms. Andrews I promise we are going to do what we can to find the suspect," Officer Mayweather said. They searched the rest of the apartment and said it was all clear.

"Gather your things and we will be waiting outside your front door."

"Thank you Officers," Hush told them. She followed me in every room I entered, making sure I was okay.

"Color, come here," she spoke softly. I walked over to her and gave her a huge hug.

"It's going to be fine, Ma. You can stay at my place as long as you need to."

"Will Black mind?" I asked.

"Nah she'll be cool with it too. She likes you."

"Cool then." I packed a week's worth of clothes, my bag of fabric, my designs for school, and my laptop. Iceland had been in my car since before the police came over. The exotic dancewear I designed was all in my trunk along with my sewing machine. I locked my door, but before leaving I wrote down Officer Thurman and Officer Mayweather's information then we left. They informed me of how to get the incident report before they pulled out of my driveway. I kept thinking, God please get me through this. I followed behind Hush on our way to her and Black's place. The next morning I was scheduled to take another final, and with everything that had occurred, I was mentally drained. I was extremely delirious; I did not know if I was coming or going. We told Black what happened, I took an aspirin, then we went to bed.

I woke up in the middle of the night because Iceland started barking. I peeped through the blinds, but I did not see a thing, so I hopped back into bed and got underneath Hush. I did not wake until the next morning. The exam was at nine so my alarm was set for eight. Wanting to get a head start, I started getting ready around 7:45. After I was dressed, I grabbed my backpack, my purse, kissed Hush and headed out the door.

"Ain't this some shit!" I said in shock. "Fuck!" Black and Hush ran outside to see what all the shouting was for.

Black said, "Damn, Color that's fucked up."

All four of my tires had been slashed.

"Okay think fast Color," I told myself. I dropped everything except my cell phone and called my Professor. I told her my problem, and asked if it would be okay if I rescheduled the final for that afternoon. She agreed. Thank God. Okay so now that's out of the way, what now? My car was parked behind Hush and her Range was parked behind Black's car, blocking both of their vehicles from being moved.

"We can try and push Color's car on the side, but it's possible her rims may get damaged," Black suggested.

"I will just call a tow truck, again." I told them. Hush put her arm around me.

"I'm sorry you have to go through this bullshit, Color. You do not deserve any of it."

I tried resisting tears, but they rolled down my face. Helpless and miserable was how I felt. Scared that I would not be eligible to graduate, I just wept.

"Thank you both for being so nice, I really do appreciate your kindness."

"No problem, Homey," Black said.

"I do this cause I love you, Ma. No need to apologize for shit. These mutha fucka's bet not get caught slipping cause I got something for they ass," Hush said.

CHAPTER 15
A Hint of Ecstasy

Graduation is finally this weekend. I am so fortunate. I made it ya'll! (laughing). Through prayer and supportive friends, I was able to complete each one of my finals, getting all A's and one B. Since I never got the chance to redo my design project, I turned it in with a few minor adjustments. My professor told me he was aware of my ability to do better, so he scored me on what potential my dress offered. I was very blessed and grateful for that. My grades were up to par and I will walk across the stage in four days. I didn't have any more unwanted surprises after all of my tires were slashed. I've had five days of peace. An alarm was installed in my home and I bought a shot gun. I know what you are thinking. "Why a shot gun, Color?" A shot gun is easy to shoot, but hard to miss your target. If anyone came into my place while I was there, they were getting hit. Mace and a box cutter were in my presence at all times, leading me to feel safe wherever I was.

Momma and Mr. John are coming on Thursday, the

day before graduation. They are still in love after four years. They were here last Christmas visiting and Momma informed me that Mr. John was diagnosed with prostate cancer. She began telling me how much she missed me and would love if I moved back to Los Angeles. I missed her also, but California was no longer a place I could call home.

On Wednesday, Hush and I went to Party City to get decorations for my party Friday night at *Tits & Wings*. Shopping of any kind excited me. Although Hush was obviously bothered by my plans of moving to New York real soon, she was proud of me for accomplishing one of my goals. Hush was awkwardly quiet and kept to herself.

"I want all white decorations, Boo," I told her. "White décor is simple yet sexy."

"Okay, Ma, get whatever you want."

We walked down every aisle while I put things I loved in the basket.

"My girls are all wearing jade green for the graduation set, too. It's going to look real nice with a white background."

"Wait, you dancing Friday night?"

"Yes, I am dancing, It's my graduation. Besides, that is the only way, I'm allowed to get money from the set."

"What is a set anyway?"

"Baby, it's when the main girl along with the dancers she's chosen gets on stage at the same time and dance. All the money that's thrown on stage is collected then given to the girl that's celebrating a birthday or graduation."

"I'm saying though, you have not danced in months," she said.

"It's okay, Baby. It's only one more night then I am saying bye to exotic dancing forever."

"That's what ya'll all say," she mumbled.

"Who the hell is ya'll?" I asked.

"Just girls in general," she replied.

"Really, Hush, you want to go there?"

"Color, it doesn't even matter. Let's just get what we need so we can run over to the club and pay for the VIP section."

"Why do we need to do that today?"

"Because Friday is graduation for other people, too, Color. You know it is first come, first serve there."

"You do not have to get an attitude damn," I said angrily.

"There you go with that flip ass mouth of yours. A nigga ain't even mean it like that," Hush said.

"Whatever, Hush, let's go!"

"Color, wait! My bad."

"Just take me home," I told her. She pulled me closer to her.

"Baby just chill. I'm sorry. Get your stuff and then we can go," Hush said. I calmed myself down quickly.

"Alright, I'm sorry, too, Hushy-Pooh."

We got everything we needed and left. She brought me home so I could clean up and prepare things for the weekend. The plan was to have a celebration dinner at *P.F. Chang's* following the graduation ceremony, so I called to verify the reservations. I also contacted Candy and Mocha to make sure they were still assisting me with decorating the club Friday morning once the club closed. They were still down.

Later that evening, Hush came by with a large supreme pizza and hot wings. I went over the plans for this weekend with her while we ate. I also showed her the black dress I was wearing underneath my gown. The dress was knee length and tight fitting. Its back was mesh down to the center of my back and the front of the dress was mesh around the neckline and chest area, which stopped just above my breasts.

"Dang, Ma. That's a sexy ass dress," Hush said.

"Thanks, Baby. I made it."

"Where you think you wearing that to?" Hush inquired.

"The graduation ceremony."

"Where you getting your degree from, the Playboy Mansion?" Hush joked.

"Whatever Hush." I replied.

"Nah, I'm just playing, Ma. That dress is hot though." She paused momentarily. "While we're on the subject, am I invited to your dinner party?" she asked.

"Yes, of course you are. Our reservations are for 3:30 pm at *P.F. Chang's*. You may have to meet me there because I will probably ride with my mom and Mr. John on campus."

"That won't be a problem. Do you mind if I invite Black?" Hush asked.

"Baby, you can bring whomever you like. Just make sure they know how to behave in public," I said jokingly.

"Ha, ha. Funny. Most of my friends know how to act," she replied.

"I hope so because my mother will call them out if they don't." We both laughed.

"Will you help me with my zipper?" I asked Hush. "It's stuck."

"Come here. I never mind helping you remove your clothes."

"I'm sure you don't mind," I told her.

Even though we had been seeing each other for a little over five months, Hush and I have only slept together a few times, but she saw me naked a hundred times. That kind of bothered me at first, but I realized over time that is just her. She never made the first move either. I guess you can't judge a person by their outside appearance. Once Hush unzipped the back of my dress, I went into my bedroom and slipped on my black lace chemise without panties.

I yelled from my bedroom into the living room while she watched television. "Meet me on my balcony."

Sometimes I would go out there to relax and read a book. That night, I had other plans. I placed my glass of red wine on the table then draped the wicker chair with my black robe before sitting. Shortly after, Hush opened the French doors and sat down on the stool in front of me while she held her Corona in her hand. It was my chance to see if she really liked me.

"What's good, Ma? Why are you sitting out here?"

"No special reason, I just felt like getting some fresh air," I lied.

"Do you always wear your lingerie out here like that?"

"Yes, when I feel like it."

"What about your neighbors? I know they can see you."

"They can't see what I'm wearing, Baby. They can hardly see me on my balcony unless I have the light on. Quit worrying, Sweetheart, we are fine." I assured her.

"Come here, Ma. You're too far away."

"I will come in a second. I want to look at you," I told her.

"Alright, Sexy," she said.

I stared at her for a minute without saying a thing.

"Hush," I said. "I'm horny." She looked at me in amazement then took a sip of her Corona.

"Let's go inside," she said. I cocked my right leg up revealing my bare shaved pussy.

"My pussy is so wet for you Hush." I stuck my middle finger in my mouth and sucked on it before aggressively inserting it inside of me. Pushing it in and out of me, my pussy juices dripped down my ass onto my robe. I heard a distant moan.

"Damn, Color, that's how you feel?"

"Yes, Hush," I said while moaning intensely. "I need you right now."

The wind was blowing and my wind chimes were singing. She walked over with her Corona bottle in her hand. Every step she took caused my pussy to throb even harder.

"Hmm, Hush," I moaned. Before breathing another breath, her lips were caressing my neck and the head of the Corona bottle was inside my contracting pussy.

"Ahh," I sighed in relief, gyrating my hips as she shoved it in and out, deeper and deeper inside of me.

"I know what you need, Ma," she whispered in my ear.

"Ooh, Hush, don't stop," I screamed. She rubbed on my erect nipples and kissed my belly button. I opened my legs wider and signaled for more.

"My dick is so hard, Ma," she said as she removed the bottle from my dripping wet pussy.

She went down and softly bit and sucked on my clit. Hush began tongue kissing my pussy lips and suddenly slipped her long tongue inside of me, tasting every drop of my love.

"Harder, Baby!" I screamed as I pushed her head further into my pussy.

"You make me feel so good," she said. "This is why we can't be doing this."

Hush got me to the point I was yearning for, then she put her finger in my asshole and made me want her even more. I kissed her cheek.

"I love the way you're handling me," I told her.

"It's not over yet, Ma," she said convincingly. "I'm about to give you what you need."

She turned me over, grabbed my hair, and slapped her dick on the back of my ass cheeks before spreading them apart.

"Fuck me, fuck me now," I moaned.

She gripped my hair with her right hand and slapped my ass with her left hand. The tighter she pulled my hair, the wilder I got. I wanted that dick so bad.

"You ready for that dick, Ma?" she asked.

"Yes, Baby! Yes!"

She spread my ass cheeks further apart and pushed the head of her dick inside me in a circular motion teasing me. I clamped my pussy on it, not wanting to let go. Hush pushed all of it inside of me, expanding my inner walls.

"Ooh. Ahh," she moaned and I moaned, too.

She stroked her dick back and forth as she slapped my booty and pulled my hair.

"That pussy for me right?" she asked.

"It's all yours, Hush."

I continued tightening my pussy muscles while she grew weaker and weaker. Hush turned me over on my back and dug deeper and deeper inside of me. She hit spots I never knew could be touched. My legs shook. I was about to cum, but before I could, Hush stood me up and bent my upper body over the rails of my balcony and fucked me harder and faster.

"Shit, I'm coming!" I screamed. My entire body began trembling shortly after. She held me tight as she came seconds later.

"I needed that," I told her. Too weak to walk, Hush carried me inside and put me in bed.

"Get some sleep, Baby. You have a long day ahead of you," she said.

"Ok, Baby goodnight." We kissed each other and I fell asleep in her arms.

CHAPTER 16
State of Shock

I awoke feeling energized, yet overwhelmed. Graduation was only a few hours away, and the more I thought about it, the more anticipation filled my heart. It had been a while since I had sex as good as last night's. Tomorrow was the big day and I planned on relocating to New York in a couple of months. Life couldn't be better. I left Hush in bed and headed to rehearsal.

On my way to campus, I stopped by the post office and picked up my mail. Then I rushed over to the library to purchase my sky blue cap and gown and to payoff my remaining graduate fees. After leaving the library, I walked through the student union into the auditorium where the ceremony was going to be held. Once seated in the auditorium, I sorted through my mail. I recognized a California postage stamp on one of the envelopes without a return address so I grew curious. Before I could open it, we were told to line up near our assigned seats.

We all watched as the graduate students walked

across the stage first. Our undergrad section had quite a while to hang out before we were called to do the walk through.

"What the hell?" I thought. It would not hurt to open my mail right here. Let's just say, it would have been best to wait until I got home. When I ripped open the envelope and unfolded the letter, I noticed it was written in red ink and signed by Mrs. Kenneth Clay.

"Mrs. Kenneth Clay? What could she want?" I said aloud. I hadn't heard from Ken in over eight years. I haven't heard anything about him since the hotel incident.

My class was directed to walk on stage before I could read even the first sentence of the letter. I placed both the ripped envelope and the letter in my purse and stood in my section along with my colleagues. Even though I was thrilled about graduating, I was anxious to see what the letter was about. That one hour of rehearsal felt like the longest hour of my entire life. I kept thinking, wondering what she could possibly want. How did she get my address? Was everything alright? Even after patiently waiting, I was unable to read it right after rehearsal because the Director of the School of Fashion asked us to meet in the dining hall for food and beverages. Two hours later, I drove home, dropped all my things on the living room table, and began reading the letter while sitting on my balcony.

Color,

I'm not sure if you remember who I am, but if you haven't forgotten about Kenneth, you haven't forgotten about me. I'm Mrs. Clay now, however, then you knew me as Phalonda, his fiancé. After his little escapade with you, Kenneth and I were married a month later. I always wondered what would have happened if I wouldn't

146

have shown up at your hotel room. Anyway, let's get to the point.

This letter is to inform you of some very alarming news. Eight years ago, Kenneth suddenly became very ill. His illness kept him from running his restaurant, so he sold it. It was difficult in the beginning with our newborn baby, but we moved away to a rural area just outside of Los Angeles. Later, Kenneth was diagnosed with HIV, which eventually turned into AIDS. He was devastated. We were all devastated. Depression took over and he decided he didn't want to live anymore. Kenneth stopped trying. He would lie in bed all day and all night. I tried to support him as much as I could during his crisis, but he was too stubborn to allow me to help. I resented him for all the years he cheated, but finally I felt sorry for him. He knew that the kids and I were HIV negative, and because of our negative results, he allowed himself to believe that God was punishing him for his lack of respect for me and our children.

On May 5th, Kenneth lost his battle. He was only 36 years old when he passed. I know you are thinking why, after all this time, would I decide to reach out to you. Well, a month ago, I tested HIV positive. My daughter is eight and KJ is eleven. It hurts to know that I may never get to see them graduate from college or even high school. Years ago I sent you an email telling you how much you reminded me of myself. Get yourself tested as soon as possible. You may not feel any symptoms now, but that doesn't mean you're clean. Good luck with your results.

Sincerely,
Mrs. Kenneth Clay

My eyes filled with tears the moment I read HIV. I knew that the letters H.I.V. and the word *good* could not be in the same sentence. I was terrified and at a loss for words. I sat there holding the letter in my hands. My legs trembled as I cried uncontrollably. I felt stupid, hopeless, sad, and weak.

"Lord, please give me the strength to get past this. I pray I do not have it. Don't let me have it," I murmured. I thought about my last pap smear being okay, but that was two years ago. Never have I been tested for HIV. My whole body grew numb, while my mind was all over the place. I wasn't sure who to call for guidance. I was in the midst of graduating and moving to start my career. This couldn't be happening right now. Not now, not ever. I cried.

All of a sudden, I remembered that sex game I played with Ken in the bathroom stall. He wasn't even wearing a condom. Why would I be so irresponsible and have unprotected sex just to make a point? Technically, it was our first time having intercourse. I should have known better. We knew better.

Usually I would have sympathy for a family infected with AIDS, but I had to deal with my own health. But wait, what if Phalonda was lying? That would be the ultimate revenge. There was no time to keep analyzing the situation. I needed to see a doctor. Hush was on her way over, but I wasn't sure what to tell her. I mean, if I was infected, she needed to know. I felt so grotesque. That was one of the reasons I preferred dating women over men. My head was hurting and my eyes were puffy, swollen, and blood shot red. I couldn't hide my emotions from her. She'd know something was wrong the second she saw me. Now was not the time to stress over this. The results wouldn't be here before tomorrow anyway, and if they were, what's the point? I argued with myself. The point was I needed to know. Momma and Mr. John were coming tonight and I hadn't cooked dinner or cleaned up.

I needed to get to a clinic and fast. I always hated going to those free clinics because everybody was in everybody else's business. I thought to myself. Phalonda said he got real sick seven years ago. We hadn't had sex in eight years. It was a 50/ 50 possibility. However, it could lie dormant for at least six months.

I went inside, washed my face, and jumped in the shower. The hot water was soothing to my body, but it wasn't putting my mind at ease. I washed my hair and turned the hot water off. There was a knock at my front door, so I wrapped a towel around the top half of my body and threw the letter in the bottom of the clothes hamper.

"That must be Hush," I thought. "She's early."

I opened the front door and no one was there. Someone had placed a broken vase with a half dozen of red roses in front of my door. I bent down to reach for the wet card that was attached to the roses and accidentally cut my finger on the broken glass.

"Fuck!" I screamed aloud.

I ran to the kitchen sink, forgetting to shut the door behind me. While I rinsed the blood from my injured finger, I heard Hush's voice.

"Color, where you at?" she said startling me.

"I'm in the kitchen," I called out. She walked into the kitchen with a curious look on her face.

"What happened, Ma?"

"I cut my finger."

"Are you alright? Let me see."

She looked at my hand and grabbed a towel from my kitchen drawer.

"Let me wrap it in this for now," she said.

Gently grabbing my hand, she tied it in the towel.

149

"Come sit down, you worrying yourself." We sat on the sofa together.

"You look like you've been crying," she asked. "Does it hurt?"

"It kind of hurts," I told her.

"Where did those flowers come from?" Hush asked.

"I don't know. I was reaching for the card, but I cut myself."

Hush got the broom and the dust pan from the kitchen.

"I will clean it up, Ma, just put some clothes on."

"Thank you," I told her.

She kissed me on my cheek and proceeded to clean up the mess. With the kitchen towel wrapped around my bloody finger, I went back and picked up the card from the kitchen floor. It read: *I still love you.*

"I really don't have the time or the patience for this shit today."

"What, Ma?"

"Huh?" I asked.

"What don't you have time for?"

"Oh nothing important, Baby," I told her. "I was reading the card and I think it's from the same person who has been stalking me."

"I thought they stopped."

I passed her the card.

"I thought so, too."

"Well maybe they are from someone who has a crush on you," Hush said.

"A crush would not send me a broken vase with flowers to my front door."

"Yeah, you are probably right, Ma."

With my heart still beating fast, I knew I had to let her know what was going on. I wanted to be as honest as possible with Hush.

"Baby, come over here and sit down," I told her. She walked over and kissed me.

"What's up?"

"There is something I need to speak to you about." I paused for a minute. "And I have something to show you."

"Okay what is it?" Hush asked.

She was so sexy. I hated to ruin things between us, but it could get worse. I took a deep breath then allowed the words to slip from my mouth.

"I received a letter from someone I knew back in Cali."

"Okay."

"It contained some perplexing information," I said.

"Where is the letter?" Hush asked.

"It's in my bathroom, I'll get it."

When I returned with the letter in my hand, I noticed a sign of worry on my Hushy-Pooh's face.

"Did anyone die?" she asked.

"No. I mean yes." As I handed her the letter, tears fell from my eyes.

"I need to throw on some clothes. I'll be right back, Hush."

With the bath towel still wrapped around me, I walked towards my bedroom to change, but there was another knock at the door.

"Shit! What now?" I wondered.

I grabbed my rain coat that hung from the coat rack and threw it on.

"Who is it?" I yelled.

"It's a surprise," a familiar voice said. I looked over at Hush and there was a puzzled expression on her face. Oh God, I guess she read the bad part. I hesitated before answering the door.

"Go ahead, answer it," she said.

I opened the door and there they were my mother, Mr. John, and Fal.

"Well, aren't you happy to see us?" my mother asked.

"Momma?" I said in awe. "What are you doing here? I thought I was supposed to get you and Mr. John from the airport later on tonight. Come on in. Fal, what a surprise." Fal smiled at me and gave me a huge hug.

"Gotcha," Fal said.

"You sure as hell did. Oh, I'm sorry everyone, this is my good friend Emery. She stood up and shook everyone's hand.

"Nice to meet you, Mrs. Andrews," Hush told my mother. "I was just leaving."

"You were?" I asked.

"Uh yeah, I have to meet up with a friend for brunch."

"Okay, well I'll walk you outside."

"It was nice meeting you all," Hush said to everyone before walking out of the door.

By then she had folded the letter up and put it in her back pocket. Once we were outside, away from the unexpected arrival of my guests, she passed the letter to me.

"So…." I said.

"So what?" she asked.

"What do you think about the letter?"

"I thought it was intriguing," she replied.

"Intriguing? Is that all you have to say?"

"Color, what do you want me to say?"

"Say what you feel! Just say something."

"We'll talk about this later. You have to see about your family and your stud friend."

"Who? Fal? Come on, Hush. Is that why you decided to up and leave?"

"I'm saying the same shit we was gon' do, she can do it with you."

"It's not even like that, Baby."

"Oh it's not? I saw the way the two of you looked at each other."

"Hush, I was surprised to see her. We have been best friends since we were like nine years old."

"Really, and how long did it take before ya'll was fucking?"

"Hush, that's not fair."

"You ain't denying it."

Before I was able to defend myself, Hush walked off from me and drove away. This was just a messed up day. It couldn't get any worse. I tucked the letter in my rain coat and went back inside. Everyone was looking at me when I walked in.

"What?" I asked them.

My mother said, "Your little friend didn't have to run off because we are here."

"No, it's fine, Momma. Mr. John, how have you been?"

"I'm hanging in there, Color," he replied.

"We are hanging in there together," Momma added.

"What do you have to eat in here," Fal asked.

"It's some food in there, but I haven't had time to get groceries. That happens when you make unannounced visits." We all laughed.

"Let's go out to eat," Mr. John suggested.

"What ya'll feel like eating?" I asked.

"Child, you have been in Louisiana way too long, talking about some ya'll," my mother joked.

"I can go for a big juicy steak," Mr. John said.

"So can I, Honey," my mother told him.

"That's fine. We can eat at *Barn's Steakhouse.*

"I prefer a more upscale steak restaurant for you ladies," Mr. John said.

"Sure, we can do *PriMos Steak and Italian restaurant.* It is really upscale, but first let me put some clothes on."

I went into my bedroom's closet, took the letter from my rain coat, and tucked it in my Steve Madden shoebox.

"Color hurry up girl," Fal said.

"I'll be ready in 10 minutes, Fal." I heard my bedroom door close. When I turned around, she was sitting on the edge of my bed. "Why did you close the door?" I asked.

"I wanted a kiss. Is that alright with you?"

"No Fal, it is not."

"That's how we go now?" she asked.

"Fal, we talked about this remember? We both agreed that we are better off as friends."

"I remember, but we can still fuck without expectations right?"

"Fal, I'm good." Even though the look on her face turned me on, I knew I had way too much drama in my life to prolong a fling with my childhood best friend.

"Do me a favor," I said.

"Whatever you want."

"Please go wait in the front." She looked at me with

a smirk on her face.

"Alright, Color, cool."

"Shut the door behind you too." She damn near broke the hinge off the door from shutting it so hard. I knew she was upset, but I didn't have time to think about her feelings right now. I could apologize to her later. I threw on a button down khaki dress with my blue and brown sandals and we went off to the restaurant.

Lunch at *PriMos* was delicious. All of us enjoyed our food. After leaving the restaurant, we went to the local casino for a little gambling and so Momma and Mr. John could have a few drinks. We all had a wonderful time. I wasn't really that into gambling, but after winning a few hundred dollars, I might be doing it more often. Fal and I had the kind of fun we used to have back in the day. Momma and Mr. John both seemed as happy as the last time they visited.

I pulled Momma aside for a moment.

"How's he really doing, Momma?"

"Who, Baby?" she asked.

"Mr. John," I said.

"He's doing much better. What about you, Color? How are you doing?"

"I'm fine, Momma. I'm excited about tomorrow and I'm just ready to start fresh in New York."

"Are you really going to move all the way on the East coast? I thought it was something you only thought about, but wasn't sure about actually doing."

"Momma, of course I'm serious. It's the best opportunity ever. I will be doing what I love to do and it is the best market for my kind of fashions."

"I understand, Baby. It's a whole lot further away than we are now."

"Momma, we can visit each other every chance we get."

"I suppose you are right."

"Everything will be okay, Momma, I promise."

Mr. John walked over and asked us if we were ready to go home.

"I think we have had enough fun for the evening," Momma told him.

My mind had calmed down quite a bit, but still there was so much that bothered me.

CHAPTER 17
Graduation Day

The day had finally arrived. The sun shined so beautifully and the smell of bacon, eggs, and French toast was pleasantly refreshing to my senses. I rolled out of bed and opened the door to my balcony. The bright sun shined on me, and I looked forward to enjoying the rest of the day. Prior to shutting the door and opening the blinds, there was a knock at my bedroom door.

"Yes?" I called out.

"Color, your moms fixed breakfast."

I almost forgot Fal was even here. "I'll be out in a minute."

"Okay, I will let her know," she said.

I brushed my teeth, pulled my hair in a ponytail and went to eat breakfast.

"Well good morning, Graduate," my mother said.

"Good morning, Momma. Good morning, Mr. John."

"Good day, Color," he said.

"Thanks, I need a good day."

"Where is Fal, Momma?" I asked.

"She's outside smoking a cigarette."

"I'm going to go check on her."

"Hurry before the food gets cold."

"Okay, Momma." I opened the door and she was sitting on the steps.

"What's up?" I asked her. "You couldn't wait until after breakfast to smoke?"

"Nah, I needed to hit it a few times. I'm right behind you."

"Okay," I told her. Fal quickly snatched my arm as I turned to enter the door.

"Color, wait. I need to talk to you."

"It has to be quick, Momma's waiting."

"It'll be brief."

"What's on your mind, Fal?"

"I can't stop thinking about you."

"Fal, we have discussed this, we can not do this. I have moved on and you need to as well. I'm sorry. I need you to be more of a friend to me right now." Tears filled her eyes when I said that.

"You are right, my fault. I wanted to tell you congratulations, you did it."

I smiled at her and wiped the tears from her face.

"Thank you. I needed to hear that from you." We hugged and went inside for breakfast.

Breakfast was delectable. Momma sure knew how to whip up that southern style French toast. Everyone started getting ready while I flat ironed my hair. I had taken my shower last night, so when I finished my hair and makeup, I slipped into my black dress, met my mother in the living room for pictures, then I decided to leave them behind because I could not risk being late. The ceremony was scheduled to begin at 10, but I had to arrive at eight thirty.

"Well, Momma, I think we took enough pictures. I need to get going before I'm late."

"We are so proud of you, Color. We will see you there."

"Thanks, Momma." She gave me a kiss on my cheek and I left. I'd planned on stopping by Hush's place on my way to campus, but she wasn't taking any of my calls. I thought maybe she was still upset over Fal. I looked in my rear view mirror a couple of times and noticed a black F-150 following me. I proceeded to drive to my destination. Once I got on the interstate, the person driving the truck sped up beside me.

"What are you doing?" I screamed as if they could hear me. "You stupid fuck!" I yelled out. They were blowing their horn aggressively as if they wanted me to pull over, but that was the last thing I would have done. Then they rolled down their dark tinted window and I immediately recognized the person driving.

"Oh my God." It was Corey. He yelled something, but I could not understand what he was screaming.

"What do you want?" I yelled out.

"Pull over, Bitch!" I heard him say.

"Bitch? What the hell is his problem?" I ignored him and sped up right past his ass. All of a sudden my phone rang. "Hello," I said.

"Pull over, Bitch!" Corey screamed into my receiver.

"What do you want, Corey?"

"Pull the fuck over now before I make you!" he yelled.

159

"What is going on? What do you want and why are you following me?" I asked.

"Why and What? Bitch, I'm following you because your nasty, trifling ass, gave me something. That's why," he said.

"What? Corey I don't have anything so what the hell are you yapping about?"

"You stupid, Bitch, you gave me AIDS!" he shouted.

I hung up in his face and started having flashbacks. It was Corey all along stalking me. I turned around and he was gone. "What if I did give him AIDS?"I was worried.

Shortly after, I took my exit and approached a red light. All of a sudden, I noticed Corey through my right side peripheral vision. There was a car in front and behind me. I was trapped. He drove faster and faster towards the passenger side of my car. Realizing he was about to run dead into me, I froze. I could not move, so I prayed. SKEWWW.......BOOM! SCREECH! CRACK. He hit me so hard, I was ejected from the vehicle. I heard people screaming and yelling. I remembered being in excruciating pain. Blood ran down my face and before long, I had blacked out.

CHAPTER 18
Truth Revealed

I opened my eyes when I heard the door squeak. A strange voice said, "Color you have a visitor."

"Who is it?" I murmured.

"It's Mrs. Andrews, your mother," he replied.

"Momma?"

"Hello, Color, how are you feeling?" she asked.

"Not good," I replied. "I have a migraine."

"Maybe you need to eat something," Momma suggested.

"I'm not hungry. It's this place. I don't like it here. It smells bad and the food is disgusting. I just hate it," I cried out, "I hate it!"

"Calm down, Color, or the nurse will give you a shot to help that un-controlling temper of yours," she told me.

"I don't have a temper, I'm fine."

"That is what you said last week before you were caught trying to slice your wrist with a piece of wood from your window pane."

"That was a mistake on my behalf, Momma. I didn't want to harm myself. I only wanted to leave."

"It would not have helped you or your situation," Momma said.

"What situation, Momma?"

"Color how can you ask me that with a straight face?" she asked. "The situation that put you in a mental asylum for three years, the situation that prevented you from accepting your degree, and I can not forget the critical significance of you sleeping with other people, when you knew you had HIV."

"Momma I told you none of those things are true. I'm honestly doing better, Momma, I promise. Now will you take me home please?"

"No, Color! You are a disgrace to our family and to yourself."

"Don't say that Momma, I'm so sorry. Just please take me home, Momma," I cried out.

"You are better off in here," she replied.

"I said I'm better," I yelled.

Then Momma told me, "You were always so obedient and jovial, but you are not that person anymore."

"I am still that person, Momma, I'm just more mature."

"Mature, Color? You are far from maturity. You're a self- centered, manipulative, corrupt, unpredictably changeable little heffa!" Momma was crying and looking at me in disgust. "I did not raise a lying whore."

"How can you say all those bad things to me?" I asked.

"Color, save the bullshit for someone else. Have you forgotten about your diary? Well, it was given to me after the court hearing. I'm aware of all your nasty, disgusting, shocking secrets. Your father would be ashamed of you if he were alive."

"My daddy loves me," I screamed. "He's all I had! Daddy loved me unconditionally!"

"And I didn't show you how much I loved you?" Momma asked. "I worked my ass off to keep a roof over our heads and you want to hold falling in love with another man against me? Well, forgive me for not drowning in sorrow. Royal would not have wanted me to be miserable. He loved me too much!" she yelled back.

I screamed from the top of my lungs, "I hate you! Fuck you, Momma! Get out stupid, Cunt! I never want to see you again!"

"Ditto," she replied.

I jumped out of bed and leaped on her back as she turned away to exit my room. "I hate you," I screamed. "You killed my daddy and you are the reason I'm stuck in this shit hole!" I scratched up her face and pulled her to the floor by her hair.

"Get this crazy bitch off of me!" my mother yelled out.

Seconds later, four men and one lady bust through the door pulled me off Momma, pinned me down, and gave me a shot in my arm. I immediately became weak and fragile. Momma stood over me and said, "If it were up to me, you'd be here for the remainder of your life." Suddenly I drifted off to sleep.

Truth Revealed continued…
Told by: Helen Andrews (Color's mother)

Color was accused of knowingly transmitting HIV to her sexual partners. Corey, the plaintiff, supplied Color's diary as evidence. After the jury declared her not guilty due to a history of lacking the capacity to realize she was committing a wrongful act, she pled not guilty by reason of insanity and was admitted to the LA Mental Health Hospital.

Although she graduated at the top of her class, the car accident prevented her from accepting her diploma. She suffered from moderate head injuries, a fractured arm, and a few cuts and bruises, but she was out of the hospital after a few weeks. Corey, however, wasn't so lucky; he was paralyzed from the waist down.

Throughout this unexpected journey, my daughter displayed an evil side of her. I was not mindful of the serious issues she possessed until passages from her diary were read aloud during the trial, most of which were profoundly unbelievable.

Here are a few things she wrote from the time she was 12 years old…

October 12, 1997
 My mom met Carlos about a year ago. He's pretty hot for an older guy, but he isn't the typical guy she would date. Momma is such a hoe. Daddy would be so upset with the stupid decisions she makes.

April 27, 1998

    Momma and Carlos got married. Ugh I hate the two of them together. Their relationship is nothing compared to she and Daddy's partnership. There has to be something I can dig up about him.

March 06, 2000

    According to a very reliable source, I found out Carlos served time for statutory rape. He is such a loser. A few see through nightgowns and rubbing my booty against his scrawny dick was all it took to convince him. I knew we would be doing it in no time. I told Momma he wasn't good enough for her, but she was too busy trying to depend on him to pay the bills; stupid ass.

November 16, 2002

    Two years after secretly fucking me, I was able to get Carlos to fuck me in my ass. Originally, he was hesitant, but he is too pussy whipped to turn me down. I am becoming sick of him fucking Momma and me so I need to find a way to get rid of him, and fast.

January 05, 2003

    If I were stupid, I'd believe I met the man of my dreams. His name is Kenneth, Kenneth Clay. He's older, the player type, but I make sure I get money from him whenever I see him. And once he gets a piece of me, he will never forget about Color.

July 26, 2003

    Recently, I found out Freeh and her husband, Kyle,

are swingers, but she has had me all to herself. Her husband wants to fuck me, too, but he shouldn't worry because he gets a part of me every time he makes love to his wife. There's nothing like a husband and wife lusting over you.

February 28, 2004
I haven't heard anything from Freeh or her husband since they moved to Atlanta. I guess after Freeh caught me and Kyle fucking in their bedroom, she had nothing more to say to me. Forget about her though. I can have anybody I want. Although she did give me incredible head.

December 24, 2005
I'm not happy here. I'm seriously considering relocating back to Louisiana. Maybe I'll find more there.

August 16, 2009
Fal came down when I got my new place. We slept together and apparently she loved it. It was good, but her body odor was atrocious. I can not do a thing with that. Smelling good is a plus and a must when you dealing with me. We are just better off as friends.

October 17, 2009
I met this guy at school named Corey. He's alright; handsome, quiet dude. I have tried avoiding men, but he has helped me pass one of my classes, so I felt obligated to show my appreciation. I wasn't trying to pussy whip his corny ass, though. It is definitely time for something new and fresh.

April 11, 2010
Dear Diary,
Sorry I've neglected you, but I have been occupied by

a chic I met. Her name is Emery, but she goes by Hush. Ooh mentioning her name moistens my panties. She is hands down the greatest person I have ever met, but I vowed never to fall in love again.

July 09, 2010
> *Dear Diary,*
> *Someone is testing my last nerve! After a few break-ins and mishaps, I need to get protection. It's probably one of Hush's lil bitches or one of them hatin' ass hoes at the club.*

That's only part of the nonsense that was exhibited to all of us in court. I was too embarrassed to even speak of Color after finding out who she truly was.

First Day of Court

"Nothing in my diary reveals that I intentionally gave anyone HIV," Color said after the prosecutor asked her about the passages from her diary.

"You are correct, Color, it doesn't, but you intentionally disguised your deceitful personality. While manipulating everyone throughout your life's history, two out of six people you've slept with are HIV positive," the prosecutor replied.

"You can't prove they contracted it from me," Color pleaded.

"That's where you're wrong. During your stay at the hospital, while you recovered from your injuries, you tested positive for HIV," the prosecutor revealed.

"I don't believe you," Color argued.

"Oh, I beg to differ, Color. I have no further

questions. You may step down."

Color took her seat while the prosecutor prepared her other notes.

"Your, Honor, I call Emery "Hush" Love to the stand."

"What? Hush?" Color said as she looked dumbfounded. She looked fearful for the first time in her life. Color watched as Emery approached the stand.

"Raise your right hand and place your left hand on the Bible," the Bailiff said, "Do you swear to tell the truth, the whole truth, and nothing but the truth, so help you God?"

"Yes I do," Emery commented.

"Emery, how do you know Color Andrews?" the prosecutor asked. Emery cleared her throat before answering.

"We were close friends."

"How close would you say the two of you were?"

"We were lovers." The voices in the audience grew overwhelmingly loud.

"Order in the court!" Judge Watson shouted.

"Can you repeat that please?" the prosecutor asked.

"We were lovers," Emery replied.

"How long had you known Ms. Andrews before the two of you made love?"

"Objection!" Color's lawyer interrupted. Judge Watson told the prosecutor to proceed.

"About a couple of weeks," Emery said.

"Interesting, and where did you meet her?"

"We met at *Tits & Wings*," Emery mumbled.

"Excuse me Emery, can you speak a little louder and repeat your last statement so that the jury can hear you."

"We met at a strip club called *Tits & Wings.*"

"Thank you." The jurors were clueless.

"Emery, how do you know the plaintiff Corey?"

"Huh," Colored said looking puzzled. "What is going on?" Color asked her defense attorney.

"Corey is my brother," Emery said. Color and the audience grew quiet.

"Corey is your brother?" the prosecutor asked.

"Yes," said Emery, reassuring everyone that what she said was the truth.

"Well, how is it that you both met Color, only on separate occasions?"

"It wasn't by coincidence," Emery shared.

"Will you elaborate further, please?" the prosecutor asked.

"Corey mentioned Color a few times and told me he was thinking about proposing to her, but then he found out she was stripping and sleeping around for money. So, he went to the doctor and got checked out which was how we found out he was HIV positive. From that day on, we planned to get revenge. Corey knew of Color's alternative lifestyle and suggested we manipulate a few things here and there," Emery revealed.

"A few things like what?"

"Nothing specific, just frighten her a bit by making her believe someone was seriously stalking her and have her fall in love with me, before leaving her alone."

"So you and Corey only wanted to teach her a lesson?"

"Yeah, something like that," Emery said.

"Tell us, Emery, what did Color receive recently, proving that her health was at risk?" the prosecutor asked.

"She showed me a letter written by the wife of one

169

of her ex- boyfriends."

"What was exactly discussed in this letter?" the prosecutor asked.

"The lady said her husband died of AIDS and that she's currently living with HIV," Emery told her.

"I have no further questions," the prosecutor said before taking her seat. Then Color's attorney approached the stand.

"Can you give us the names of the victims listed in this infamous letter?" Color's attorney asked Emery.

"No, I can't remember their names."

"How do we know the letter even exists?"

"Because I read it," Emery replied.

"You can not prove you read it, nor can you prove that my client purposely gave your brother HIV."

"My brother showed me his results after he suspected he could have possibly gotten an STD from Color." Emery was unable to finish her sentence.

"She is lying, Your Honor," the defense attorney said.

"I never planned for it to go this far. After I read the letter, I knew I couldn't go through with what we had planned." Emery said.

"What did you have planned, Emery?"

"Objection, Your Honor," Corey's lawyer shouted.

Judge Watson said, "Proceed."

"What was the plan?"

"We wanted her to suffer," Emery said crying. "The car accident was too much for me to deal with. I never wanted to physically hurt my brother or Color. We only wanted Color to pay for what she had done. She ruined our lives. My brother is all I got left."

"Fuck you, Hush! You ate my pussy, you probably

have it too," Color cried out to her, "You can not sit there and tell me you don't love me!"

"Order in the court," Judge Watson shouted.

Officers removed Color from the courtroom and a retrial was scheduled. During the first few months of awaiting trial, Color attempted to take her life on five different occasions.

I'm not sure where I went wrong or if it would have even been possible for me to have done more to prevent all of this from happening. I understood that most of the frustration came from losing her father, Royal. All along, I was teaching her to be on the lookout for cunning people, but I should have been keeping a close eye on her. She played both parts, the innocent role and the sly role. As Color's mother, I can only love both sides of her.

CHAPTER 19
A Different Color

I never thought that during my spirit of hedonism, I would become completely dejected. The execution of my plan to find happiness backfired. My challenges were greatly conducive to the study and craft of deceiving those who crossed my path. Personally, I thought there was not enough information to successfully incriminate me. Hell, I'm Color Jade "Persuade" Andrews. My beauty naturally captivates people and they gravitate towards my mysterious smile. It wasn't difficult having my way at all.

My unquestionable probity has helped me lure everyone in my life and have them right where I intended. Given their approbation to be enamored by yours truly, I let the games begin. Carlos, Freeh, and Freeh's husband, Kyle, were all my paramours before I became saturated with boredom. My relationships between Ken and Hush were most exciting. They were both sexy and wealthy, which always put a smile on my face, and my pussy.

One thing is for certain. Contracting HIV was not in my plans. When I became aware of my status, I made arrangements to move back to Louisiana. Upset and confused, I became a different person. The heavy plotting began. My purpose was to live life to the fullest, even if it meant passing on my virus.

The car accident hindered my participation in my graduation ceremony and postponed my plans of moving to New York. I was out of the hospital in no time. Unfortunately, I was subpoenaed by Corey weeks later. I had to play crazy to get off in court. I explained the heavy impact my father's death had on me throughout my troubling life. I pleaded to them, "How could I live a healthy life without my father?" I said. "He was my heart, my reason to look forward to my future. I've had psychological counseling and medication, but still I'm emotionally distracted by the death of my father. I didn't get annual check-ups. How could I have known I had AIDS?" I asked the prosecutor as I cried. The jurors felt my pain and because of my Oscar winning performance, I pled insanity. Now I'm stuck in a damn psychiatric hospital until I get "better." I have to admit, this is a whole lot better than prison. Thank goodness I didn't reveal Carlos' murder in my diary or I would have been screwed. Corey wanted me dead, but because of his unfortunate paralysis, I still get the last laugh.

www.ingramcontent.com/pod-product-compliance
Lightning Source LLC
Chambersburg PA
CBHW021232090426
42740CB00006B/503